The Carpet
Weaver of
UŞAK

ALSO BY KATHRYN GAUCI

The Embroiderer

Conspiracy of Lies

Seraphina's Song

The Carpet Weaver of UŞAK

KATHRYN GAUCI

First published in 2018 by Ebony Publishing
ISBN:
Paperback: 978-0-6481235-4-5
Ebook: 978-0-6481235-5-2

This book is dedicated to the Asia Minor Refugees and to all those who saw their way of life destroyed in Anatolia, regardless of which side they belonged to. They are all casualties of the irrationality of war and its effect on the human condition.

On a personal level, this book is also dedicated to my husband, Charles, for his unwavering support, and to the memory of my parents, who gave me the freedom to pursue my dreams.

Note on Turkish spelling and names

As this novel is set in Anatolia, I have kept authentic Turkish names. Most Turkish letters are similar in pronunciation to their English counterparts, but some are unique to Turkish. The following presents the Turkish letters with the sounds they correspond to in English.

C (as in jade)	Cemal = Jemal
Ç (ch as in church)	Çanakkale = Chanakkale, Bekçi Baba = Bekchi Baba, Mecnun Dede Mosque = Mechnun Dede Mosque, Cemal Paşa = Jemal Pasha
Ö (as in bird)	Ömer
Ş (sh as in shoe)	Uşak = Ushak, Pınarbaşı = Pinarbashi, Ayşe Baci = Ayshe Baji, Sarıkamış = Sarikamish, Hoş geldin = Hosh geldin, Maşallah = Mashallah
Ü (as in cute)	Süleyman

"In their memory, I sing with sadness, Lord.
Were you made of stone, you would spill tears for them."

Mustafa Tabti. Algerian War Poet.

Contents

CHAPTER 1

The Loquat Tree

Nea Ionia, Athens 1970

Christophorus stood by the bedroom window looking at the loquat tree in the garden. The tree was his pride and joy. He planted it when he moved there over thirty years now; so long ago he couldn't recall the exact date. What he did know was that when he looked at it, he didn't just see a beautiful tree with glossy green leaves; he saw a little patch of Anatolia under the Athenian sky. It served to remind him of his former home; the one far away in a land that he would never set foot in again. It's thanks to the loquat tree, that not a day passed when he did not recall with a heavy heart, the happy years of his youth and a life he thought would never change.

Throughout the long, hot summer months, he watched its tiny buds develop into small clusters, until finally, when the first autumn chill cooled the last summer breeze, the clusters burst open revealing small, creamy-white flowers, and releasing a fragrance so sweet that it permeated the entire garden. When it became too cold to sit outside, he continued to observe the tree from his bedroom window. Each spring, the tree was a mass of succulent orange-fleshed fruit, and the cycle was complete.

It was during the flowering of the loquat tree that he first felt her presence, and he remembered every detail about that day. Alone in his room, a hand touched his shoulder, so soft that at first he thought he was imagining things. Then it happened again and he turned to look behind him, but there was no-one there. What did he expect? If there had been someone, he would have seen them in the mirror. All he saw was his own face, a man in the twilight of his years. Next came the scent; musky, oriental, sensuous. A scent he would remember till the day he died. It was *her* scent. He closed his eyes and inhaled. Repressed memories flooded back. When he opened them again he saw her face in the mirror next to his. She was exactly the same as the last time he saw her — young and beautiful.

The days passed into weeks and then months, and all the time he hoped and prayed Aspasia would return, just as she had that afternoon. When he least expected it, he felt her presence once again. This time he was shaving in front of the mirror and the radio was playing a Mitsakis number. He took a few steps backwards, bumping into a small table and knocking over a silver-framed photograph. Her face remained there and he pinched himself hard. This was not a dream. Then he heard her voice.

'Not even death will part us, my love.'

They were the same words she had said to him time and time again. But they were not the last words she uttered on that fateful night. The rest he had blocked out in order to carry on. Now he heard her whisper those words again.

'A child that cries will give you away,' she said. 'For the sake of the others, think carefully.'

And then she was gone. He touched the mirror where her image had been.

'Aspasia,' he cried out, his body still trembling from shock. 'Aspasia! Don't leave me. Stay a while longer. Aspasia!'

When he realised she was no longer there, he slumped on the bed with his head in his hands, sobbing like a child. After all these years, she had finally kept her promise never to leave him, but why now? Her memory and the events of that last day together tumbled around his mind. He heard screams, smelt the blood-soaked earth, but most of all, he heard the cry of a new-born.

There was a knock on the door and Elpida entered.

'*Papa*, are you alright? I heard you talking to yourself.' She sat on the bed and put her arms around him. 'What on earth is it? Shall I call the doctor?'

'It's nothing, my daughter. I don't know what came over me. I'll be alright soon.'

Elpida wasn't convinced. She noticed the frame lying face down on the floor and picked it up.

'The glass has cracked,' she said. 'We'll have to buy another.'

It held a photo of her as a small child, together with her mother, and it was one of their most treasured possessions.

'How old was I when this was taken?' Elpida asked, wiping the frame carefully with her handkerchief.

'You had just had your first birthday,' her father replied.

She put the photo back in its place on the crocheted doily. 'Come on, Papa, let's go in sit in the garden and I'll make you a coffee.'

Christophorus reached for his walking stick. Perhaps she was right. The fresh air would do him good.

Elpida covered the rectangular table with a plastic checked tablecloth, secured the corners with wooden pegs, and placed a vase of loquat blooms in the centre. Sunlight streamed through the outer branches of the tree creating a flickering, hypnotic dance on the paving. At this time in the afternoon it was peaceful and the only sounds those of the cicadas and the random clatter of a pot from someone's kitchen. Later in the evening, the peace would be broken by a muffled cacophony of sounds from nearby houses; televisions, radios, and the occasional family argument that no one was meant to overhear. All this permeated the neighbourhood into the early hours of the morning. Amidst these haphazardly built white-washed homes with their uneven roofs and coloured doors, the rituals of daily life came and went, and the years passed with very little change from one to another.

Christophorus didn't mind. It gave him a feeling of security, and security was what he and the other refugees craved, even now, almost fifty years after leaving their homeland. Those *Anatolides* or *Tourkomerides*, as the local Greeks like to call them, were peace-loving people and devoted to their families. They rarely made trouble and in return, had garnered respect from the old Greeks.

Elpida came outside with a tray of Greek coffee and a plate of *revani*.

'I made it this morning, especially for you,' she said, cutting a large slice of the syrup-drenched sponge and placing it in front of him, 'and for Christos. It's one of his favourites too.'

Christos was his grandson, Elpida's son, and he was named

in honour of his grandfather. Christophorus had helped to raise him as both of Elpida's husbands had died young; the first in the war against the Germans, and the second of an incurable illness. He was without a wife, and his daughter was without a husband. With no money to speak of, Elpida and Christos moved in with him. It was like old times, and he and his daughter grew dependent on each other.

'How's the carpet coming along?' Christophorus asked, after a while.

'It's almost finished: another week or so at the most.'

'Do you intend to sell it like the others?'

'Yes, Papa, and this will be my last.'

It was not what he expected to hear.

'You're not the only one who is growing old, you know,' she said, with smile. 'I'm getting rather tired myself these days, and my back is playing up again.'

'But you're such a skilled weaver; it would be a pity not to continue. Besides, it runs in our blood. Who will continue after we've gone? Certainly, not Christos. That sort of work is not for a man.'

Elpida saw the disappointment on his face.

'I know it's not what you want to hear, but it's time to acknowledge that we've reached the end of the line. No one wants to do this work any longer. The young prefer to buy machine-made carpets. They are much cheaper.'

'Bah!' What kind of talk is that? There is no comparison.'

'I agree, but that's the way it is. Some of the traditions we tried to hold on to belong to another era. This is one of them.'

'Perhaps Christos will marry a weaver,' Christophorus said, hopefully. 'There are plenty of families around here with daughters who grew up with their mothers and grandmothers as weavers. Surely some of them must want to carry on this skill.'

'Wishful thinking, Papa. Do you know what young girls are like these days? They all want office jobs. Besides, it doesn't pay any longer. We are only doing it for the love of it. Anyway, Christos is still young. It will be a while before he marries. Things will be different by then I should imagine. '

'It saddens me to hear you talk like this, my daughter; you of all people. Surely women still embroiderer? Don't tell me they've lost that skill also.'

'Embroidery, yes; that's different.'

'What's so different? It's a craft that requires great skill isn't it? Besides, carpets have always been valued as part of a girl's dowry.'

'Embroidery can be carried around in a bag when the girls visit each other. You can't do that with a loom,' Elpida laughed. 'Look at me. My heavy loom takes up most of my bedroom. There's barely space for me to walk between that and my bed.'

'So are you trying to tell me that carpet weaving will soon be a lost art?' he asked, despondently. 'What would your mother think if she heard you talk like this?

'I think she would understand,' Elpida replied, and started to clear the table.

At the mention of Aspasia, Christophorus felt a chill run down his spine.

'You've gone pale again, Papa. Why don't you come and sit with me while I weave? It's been ages since you did that.'

By the time he joined her, Elpida was already sitting at the loom with her back towards him, beating down a row of knots. He sat in the old, upholstered chair next to the loom and watched. She was right when she said her loom took up too much room. There was barely enough room to swing a cat around. The loom on which she worked was the same one he'd built for her when she moved into the house. It was the vertical type, made from heavy wood with a roller beam at the bottom and a specially made screw that served to tighten the weft to the perfect tension. The weft was made of cotton stretched between the upper and lower beam, and the pile was made of wool. For this particular carpet, Elpida had chosen to use a weft of finely spun, natural wool rather than cotton. The loom almost reached the ceiling and straddled the width of a wall with barely enough space for his chair. Most importantly there was adequate light, even though the window was small.

Elpida reached up and pulled down a piece of yellow wool from one of a row of coloured woollen balls that hung across the loom, deftly twisted it around two wefts, pulled it through the centre in a loop and cut it with a sharp knife. They called it a Turkish knot, the same knot that had been used for centuries throughout Central Asia and Turkey. She counted each knot as she moved along the row: three yellow, one madder, two indigo, one cream, two indigo again, and so on, until she came to the end of the row. She dropped the knife in her lap and took up the weft, threading it first through to the left and then back to the right. After that, she picked up the heavy beating comb and beat it into place. Finally she reached for her carpet shears onto which was attached an adjustable metal strip for the desired height of the pile, and cut along the row. The unwanted wool fell into a heap on the floor, leaving a smooth velvet pile of skilfully woven motifs whose origins were lost in time.

7

A sketch of the carpet lay on the seat beside her. She picked it up and examined it to check she had followed it correctly. It had been carefully drawn onto squared paper by Christophorus and each square represented a knot. She counted aloud and then checked her work.

'Perfect,' she said. 'Not a knot out of place.'

'It's beautiful,' Christophorus replied. 'Your mother would be proud of you. Perhaps you should think carefully about selling it. You may regret it.'

'I need money for Christos's university fees. Selling it will help enormously.'

She arched her back and moved her elbows back and forth to loosen up her body. The pain of sitting at a loom for years on end was etched across her brow. It was something Christophorus was used to. Eventually, the months and years of carpet weaving took its toll on all the weavers.

'Perhaps I can help with his fees. I have a little put by, you know. That way you can keep this carpet and maybe even give it to him when he marries. If it's to be your last, I would like it to stay in the family. I think it's important. It's our heritage.'

Elpida looked at him. 'Let me give it some thought. At the moment I have other things to think about. Christos is coming tonight. He's working on a new project at the university. Something about Asia Minor and he wanted you be here.'

'And where else would I be?' Christophorus asked,

'At the kafenion playing backgammon, that's where,' she laughed.

Christophorus let out a long sigh. He was not really in the mood to talk about Asia Minor. The subject always sent him spiralling into melancholia. Elpida was aware of this and had long learned to avoid mentioning it, but tonight was different. She had no idea what it was about, but Christos said it was important.

'Take a nap, Papa. By the time you wake, the table will be filled with your favourite foods.'

*

It was seven o'clock in the evening when Christophorus awoke from his siesta. He looked forward to Christos's visits, but these days they were few and far between. He always seemed so busy with some project or other. He dressed in a smart suit and tie for the occasion. By the time he was ready, the aroma of grilled lamb cutlets wafted across the garden into his room.

Christos stood up and gave his grandfather a big hug. 'Good to see you, *Papou*. You're looking well.'

'Bah! Don't give me that,' Christophorus replied, taking a seat and inspecting the array of food on the table. 'I'm as old and gnarled as an ancient olive tree.'

Elpida lifted out a stuffed green pepper from a large tray, put it on his plate, and then made a place on the table for the lamb cutlets.

'Christos has been telling me all about his project,' she said, giving them both a large chunk of bread. 'It sounds exciting.'

She looked across at her son and nodded as if to tell him it was alright to speak. Knowing his grandfather's reticence to speak about his past, he hesitated. Christophorus sensed this and broke the ice.

'Well then, when are you going to tell me what it is, or is it a guessing game?' he said, taking a bite of cutlet.

'I'm making a documentary. It's about the Greeks in Asia Minor. When it's finished, we hope to send it to the Greek Diaspora around the world. Until now, most of what we've heard has been propaganda, and I am convinced there is another side to all this: a more balanced side. The time is right to revisit it.'

Christos and Elpida exchanged glances as they watched Christophorus's reaction. He finished his cutlet and helped himself to another stuffed pepper.

'And you want to ask me some questions. Is that it?' he replied, matter-of-factly.

'Yes, *Papou*. I've read many books, listened to speakers, heard the survivor's stories, but there always seems to be something missing; something more personal. Maybe it's because I am the son of a *refugee*, and yet I know nothing about our life there. I know you don't like to talk about the past but...' he thought about his words carefully. 'It's just that I feel as though a part of me is missing. Filling in the blanks will not only do me a world of good, it will give me the impetus I need to succeed.'

Elpida held her breath. Her father had not been himself just lately and she wondered whether it was a wise decision to open old wounds. For a while, no-one said anything. Christophorus finished his food, wiped his mouth and his thick moustache, and pushed his plate away. Elpida and Christos gazed at him in apprehension.

'You are right, my boy. Old age has taught me that it's important to know where you came from. It's a part of what makes us who we are, and I have been selfish in keeping it from you. Please forgive me. Perhaps it's not too late to make amends.'

Elpida breathed a sigh of relief, and she got up to give him a big hug. Embarrassed, he shooed her away. She brought out a fine bottle of wine that she had been saving for a special occasion, and could think of no better time to open it than now.

'What do you want to know?' Christophorus asked.

'Perhaps we can begin with the time you met *Yiayia*,' replied Christos. That should do fine. I can fill in the rest myself.'

Christophorus's thoughts drifted back to a few hours earlier. Aspasia's presence had unsettled him. The more he asked himself why she had appeared in this strange waking dream, the more he felt a sense of unease. Yet he was sure she was here with him now; maybe even listening into the conversation. He must open up for her sake. It would be what she wanted.

'That's an excellent place to start,' he replied.

Christos asked if he could tape record it all. His grandfather thought it a good idea.

Christophorus closed his eyes for a moment and took a deep breath. In that moment, he smelt the earth and tasted the air of his beloved Anatolia.

CHAPTER 2

The Beginning of the End

Bursa, June 1914

Christophorus Plato Stavrides walked into Nurettin's Kebab House opposite the Koza Han, for one last meal before returning to his home near Uşak. The Kebab House was small and unpretentious — one might even say, rather dilapidated and in need of refurbishing — but it was, never-the-less, a great favourite with the local silk merchants, and as usual, it was filled to capacity. Christophorus's long relationship with Nurettin always guaranteed him a seat in a prominent position overlooking the entrance to the han, and besides, he tipped generously. A good friend in the Ottoman Empire's silk capital was to be valued and looked after, and Nurettin had certainly been indispensible in getting him contacts which otherwise would have eluded him.

'Your table is ready, my friend,' said Nurettin, bowing slightly and at the same time gesturing towards the only empty table in the room.

Christophorus edged his way through the busy restaurant

and seated himself at a small table next to the low window ledge on which stood several narghiles and ornate copper ewers arranged in a neat row on a narrow length of brightly coloured cloth. A young boy appeared carrying an armful of small hand-towels and a ewer containing lemon water. Christophorus cupped his hands together and the boy tipped a few drops of the sweet-smelling water into them in order that he should clean them before eating. After rubbing his hands together quickly, he wiped them on the towel and handed it back to the boy who moved on to the next customer. The subtle fragrance of lemons lingered in the air.

Nurettin bent over and whispered in his ear. "I fear today is not an auspicious one, my friend.'

'Why is that?' Christophorus asked.

Nurettin gestured towards the other customers. Most were busily eating and at the same time appeared to be absorbed in reading the newspapers.

'Haven't you heard?'

'Heard what?'

Nurettin went to the counter and brought back an English newspaper.

'It's all I have left, I'm afraid. The Greek and French ones have all gone and I know you don't read Turkish.' He placed the newspaper on the table and tapped on the headline with his index finger.

ASSASINATION

OF THE

AUSTRIAN HEIR AND WIFE
SHOT BY STUDENT IN BOSNIAN CAPITAL

TWO ATTEMPTS DURING A PROCESSION

Another article was headed:

HAPSBURG DISASTERS
EMPEROR'S LIFETIME OF MISFORTUNE
DEFEATS AND DEATHS

The opening lines read —

"The Hapsburgs have produced many lunatics and one great statesman, the Emperor Charles V, but their modest capacities have not prevented their holding a high place, often the highest, in Europe for 800 years."

The article was accompanied by an artist's grisly rendition of the assassination.

'Such a terrible thing,' Christophorus said, after he had read it.

'Indeed! God preserve us that this doesn't get out of hand,' replied Nurettin.

'Why should it? What business is it of ours?'

Nurettin sighed. 'My dear friend, you work with foreigners and you know their ways better than any of us. These things have a way of escalating and before we know it, another war has cast its blood-sucking tentacles around us.'

Christophorus thought Nurettin's reaction a little over dramatic. At the same time there did seem to be an unusual air of disquiet in the room

'Surely not! The perpetrator of this abominable act — what did they say his name was?' Christophorus looked at the newspaper again. 'Gavrilo Princip — a mere student, 'he continued, 'who no-one has heard of, will be executed and that will be the end of it. Mark my words.'

'Let's hope you're right, Kyrios Christophorus. We can well do without another war. Anyway, enough of sombre thoughts, you must satisfy your appetite before you leave our good city.'

A few minutes later, a plate of tender lamb kebabs on a bed of creamed aubergine puree accompanied by chilli tomato paste and chewy bread, was placed in front of him. Christophorus tucked into them with relish.

'I will miss your food when I return to Uşak,' he said, when it came time to leave.

Nurettin clasped his hands together in the manner of one who felt greatly honoured. Christophorus would not only miss the food, he would miss his friend too. Nurettin, with his red fez and large, blackened moustache which gave him the air of an esteemed agha, had taken him in hand since he first came to Bursa almost eight years earlier, the same year he began work with The Anatolian Carpet Manufacturers Ltd. In those days he had been a mere clerk, but he did possess an eye for fine carpets of exceptional beauty and was a quick learner when it came to choosing the best materials available. As a consequence, his aptitude was noticed by his superiors and he was soon promoted. Now he traversed the length and breadth of Anatolia on behalf of the company. Through sheer hard work and dedication, Christophorus's star was on the ascent.

'Before I leave, there is something I need to ask,' he said. 'My new bride, Aspasia, I have purchased several gifts for her, but would like something rather special. You have a wife and two daughters; can you suggest anything?'

Nurettin thought for a few seconds and then gave a broad smile. 'I know just the thing. My friend, Davit Sarkissian, the Armenian shoemaker, has just received a delivery of silk slippers. My wife tells me they are the latest fashion, and that all the ladies in the Sultan's harem are wearing them. Such a beautiful gift will mean so much to a young bride.'

'An excellent idea. I am sure she would be very happy indeed to have such a pair. It is most considerate of you to think of it. Where can I find your friend? I will pay him a call straight away.'

Nurettin wrote down the name and address. 'It's not far from here; a few streets past the Mecnun Dede Mosque.'

Christophorus paid his bill, tipped handsomely as always, and promised to call again the next time he visited Bursa.

'May God go with you,' said Nurettin.

The friends shook hands and Christophorus stepped outside into the glare of the afternoon sun and walked in the direction of the Emir Han. At the corner of the dusty street, he turned left and walked a short distance until he reached the mosque. The shoe shop was at the end of a shaded side street next to a tiny cafe outside which sat three Turks smoking narghiles.

Davit Sarkissian was arranging a pair of women's velvet, gold-embroidered ankle boots on a glass stand in the window.

'What can I do for you, sir,' he asked, looking over the top of his wire-rimmed spectacles.

'I have been told that you have recently acquired a stock of the latest fashions in silk slippers. I would like to see them,' Christophorus replied.

Davit Sarkissian pushed the glasses back on his nose and walked towards the counter. On it were several pairs of slippers, each pair laid out on a small square of cloth. He picked one slipper up and held it in the palm of his hand.

'They arrived a few days ago and I am sure you will agree, they are exquisite. I purchased the silk and embroidery materials myself here in Bursa and had them made in Constantinople. My family have been shoemakers to the Sultan's family for several generations. Such high-quality workmanship you will not find anywhere else in the empire.'

Christophorus looked at them all. As a man with an eye for beauty and quality, he could not fault them. They were all stylish.

'May I?' he asked, and picked them up one by one and examined them. First the mustard yellow pair embroidered in silver-gilt thread with floral motifs, next the open-backed crimson pair embroidered with a large bird motif entwined in foliage, and so on. They were all beautiful and he was spoilt for choice. Seeing his dilemma, Davit offered to help.

'Tell me, sir, what colour is the good lady's hair?'

'As black as a raven,' Christophorus replied, wondering what the colour of hair had to do with a pair of slippers.

'And her eyes, what colour are they?'

'As dark as the finest Arabian coffee'

'And her complexion?'

'As soft and as delicate as a ripe peach,'

'And the good lady's stature? Is she tall or short?'

'A head shorter than myself,' Christophorus answered, beginning to feel uncomfortable with Davit's questions. 'With a physique as lithe as a gazelle,' he added.

He wasn't sure why he added that last statement and blushed with embarrassment.

'Excellent. One more question. 'Can you describe her ankles?'

'As delicate as a rose sapling,' replied Christophorus, thinking of the last time he glimpsed Aspasia's shapely legs underneath her nightgown.

Davit snapped his fingers. 'Perfect. I have just the right pair.'

He pushed the existing pairs aside and pulled out another wrapped in a green cloth.

'These, sir, are the slippers for your good lady.'

Christophorus drew a deep breath when he saw them. They were even more beautiful than the others. The slippers had uppers made of cream-coloured satin, embroidered with floral motifs in silver wire, sequins and beads, and decorated with a bow of self patterned silk ribbon. They were open at the back with pointed toes, curved heels and leather soles. The heels of wood were also covered in satin. Christophorus was lost for words. Davit had not even asked Aspasia's shoe size, yet he knew these would fit perfectly. He ran his fingers over the embroidery in amazement.

'I congratulate you, sir. They are magnificent. I couldn't have chosen better myself. I will take them.'

Davit smiled. 'You have excellent taste, sir. They are the finest in the collection. Your wife will wear them with pride.'

CHAPTER 3

Aspasia

Aspasia had been sitting on a raised platform by the window waiting for Christophorus to return since midday. It was now nightfall and she was beginning to worry. She knew he would have called at The Anatolian Carpet Manufacturers Ltd. before coming home, and by her reckoning, he should have been back by now. The village wasn't far from Uşak but the road was rough and pot-holed and just lately there had been several incidents of banditry in the area. A sudden terror swept through her. What if he had been killed? She tried to shake such thoughts from her head. Most likely he would be travelling with others who were also returning to the surrounding villages and there was safety in numbers.

She opened the slatted window of the protruding balcony and looked up at the dark sky streaked with irregular luminous bands of stars. What was it Christophorus had said the Greeks called it — *Kiklios Galaxious* — The Milky Way. Whatever it was, it was magnificent. She breathed in the warm night air, redolent with the fragrance of jasmine and orange blossom, and let her eyes wander down the narrow street towards the meydan.

The soft lights of the coffee houses flickered like fireflies in the night. Apart from the lights and the darkened shapes of a cluster of houses that clung haphazardly to the hillside, there was no-other sign of life. The village was silent.

Aspasia reflected on how different her life had become since she married Christophorus a few months earlier. He was her world now: he and their village, Stavrodromi. Her family was from the town of Uşak itself and when Christophorus asked for her hand in marriage, it worried her parents greatly that their only daughter would be lonely in a small village that the rest of the world seemed to have forgotten. Had it not been for the fact that Christophorus's own mother lived nearby and the family owned the large plot of land on which the house had been built, albeit as part of a dowry for his sister who unfortunately had died before she could marry herself, Aspasia's parents would certainly have turned him down.

It was at The Anatolian Carpet Manufacturers Ltd. that Christophorus first met Aspasia. A batch of dyed wool had just arrived and it was his job to distribute it to one of their factories. Aspasia was only one of many girls he saw during the course of his work but there was something special about her. She was one of those beauties who strike the heart straight away, and even though her head was bowed and her eyes lowered, he could see she radiated warmth and intelligence. Before she had finished collecting her skeins of wool, he decided she was the woman he would marry. From that moment on, he found as many excuses as he could to be near her. Did the weavers need more madder or indigo yarn? Did the carpet shears need sharpening, and so on? Every time he entered the weaving shed where she worked, he stole a glimpse in her direction.

Aspasia in turn, fell for Christophorus's dashing style. Despite his youth, his overall appearance revealed the confidence of someone who knew what he wanted out of life. She was also attracted to his fully-fledged manliness. He was a man who could give her pleasure, care for her and give her children. To all who knew them, it was evident this was a love match and after coming out to inspect their daughter's potential new home in Stavrodromi for themselves, Aspasia's parents gave them their blessing. The couple were married in the Orthodox Church in Uşak. There followed a brief honeymoon in Smyrna, paid for by the company as a wedding gift, and then they returned to Stavrodromi to begin a new life together. The future had never looked rosier.

At this point it should be pointed out that although it might have looked to the outside world that there was only one village, there were actually two. The other half of the village was inhabited by Turks. They named their village Pınarbaşı — Fountainhead — because of the free-standing fountain in the meydan which marked the division between the two villages, whereas the Greeks named their village, Stavrodromi — Crossroads — because of the roads that crossed through it. The road to the left led to the Greek village; the road to the right, to the Turkish; the road to the north, to Uşak and Kütahya, and the road to the south, Denizli and Antalya. Both villages were joined by a tree-lined meydan with a coffee house on either side with the eye-catching Fountain of the Sun and Moon in the centre.

The fountain was the life blood of both villages and was a meeting place for everyone. It was built sometime before the end of the nineteenth century by the owners of the two coffee houses, a Greek and a Turk, who decided to get together and donate money in the form of an endowment for the pleasure and use of both communities. The fountain was the result of their friendship. Prior to that, water was supplied by a small spring at the base of the hill where the hamam now stood. Opposite the hamam stood the old han, a dilapidated caravanserai now used to house the villager's horses, donkeys, mules, camels, and the occasional cow.

An architect and stonemason from Smyrna were hired to design the new fountain, and after much discussion involving the inhabitants of both villages, they came up with an elegant design in the form of a pavilion with a hexagonal base. The base was carved in a Baroque design in keeping with the newer European architectural styles, whilst the central pavilion featured four lion's heads from whose mouths the water flowed. Above the lion's heads were incised images of the sun and moon over which were inscribed the names of the cafes. The Sun Coffee House, belonging to the Greek proprietor was inscribed in Greek, and the Coffee House of the Moon, belonging to the Turkish proprietor, was inscribed in flowing Ottoman script. Elsewhere in the Ottoman Empire, relationships between the Christians and Muslims were sometimes strained to breaking point, especially after the Balkan Wars, but for the villagers of Stavrodromi and Pınarbaşı, they had never been better.

Much of this was to do with a common interest — carpet weaving. Both the Christian and Muslim women had been carpet weavers for generations and their skills were passed down from mother to daughter for as long as any of them cared to remember. The village may have appeared sleepy to the outside world, but to those in the know, it produced some of the finest carpets in Anatolia. All the women in Christophorus's family were carpet weavers, as were Aspasia's. Whilst Christophorus's family worked from home, Aspasia's worked in the new work-shops in Uşak. In the end it didn't matter where they worked, as long as they had access to the best materials, quality carpets could be woven anywhere. Aspasia was proof of that. She knew how to knot carpets before she could read.

Her earliest recollections were of sitting on a low platform next to her mother and grandmother, studying the paper designs and copying the swift movements of the grownups. By the time she started school, her nimble fingers were adept in forming the centuries old Turkish knots of her ancestors who had lived in the empire for generations. A few years later, she could memorize a simple carpet pattern with ease. For women like Aspasia, carpet weaving was like breathing. It was in their blood.

During her school years, Aspasia worked on the loom at home with her *Yiayia*, her grandmother. The moment her school years were over, she applied for a position as a weaver in one of the factories in Uşak where her mother worked. The pay was better. The more knots you could weave in an hour, the more money you earned, whereas at home, the pay was dependant on the carpet and as such was a set price. It was really up to the weaver how long they would take. Aspasia's grandmother was growing old and as a consequence was much slower. She valued her grand-daughter's help as it meant the carpets would be woven much faster. When Aspasia went to work in the factory, she missed her company and soon gave up the will to weave, complaining that her back ached from years of sitting at a loom. Nothing Aspasia or her mother could do helped. One day they arrived home to find her lying on her bed. At first they thought she was asleep but quickly realised she was dead. What's more, she knew her time was over as she had carefully wrapped her carpet tools, which comprised of a small sharp knife, a heavy beating comb and special carpet shears, and placed them next her loom along with a note on which was written:

For Aspasia from Yiayia.

Yiayia was not old but she was worn out. Years of carpet weaving did that to them. Nevertheless, it was their life, and without it they had nothing else.

Aspasia sat back on the cushion and picked up her embroidery, a gift she was making for Christophorus to use at work. It was a document holder in dark red leather with silver metal thread couched over narrow cardboard scrolls. This was the first time she had made such a thing and it wasn't easy. Her fingers ached from piercing the needle through the leather. All it needed now were his initials and it would be finished. She held the cardboard tightly in place and little by little, covered it in the shiny metallic yarn. It might have given her a few blisters, but it was worth it. More to the point, he was worth it, and that was all that mattered.

After a while, she heard the sound of approaching footsteps coming up the street. Christophorus had finally returned. She threw down her embroidery, made the sign of the cross and hurried to the door.

Christophorus was tired, yet the sight of Aspasia dressed in her flowing silk robe, ignited a fire in his belly. He cupped her face in his hands, looked into her dark, seductive eyes and gave her a long, lingering kiss.

Aspasia reciprocated his passion. 'Light of my eyes, fire of my soul, I have thought of nothing but you,' she said in a hon-eyed voice. 'Come, tell me all about your trip.'

She prepared him a light supper of *hoşmerim*, a sweet dish of Anatolian origin better known by its colloquial name as

Something Nice for the Husband, and sat next to him on a cushion whilst he ate. Just to have him back home and listen to him talk delighted her. After he had eaten, Christophorus presented her with her gifts; a pair of gold earrings in a filigree design, a box of *marrons glacés* — a speciality of Bursa, several lengths of silk cloth, and an assortment of coloured ribbons, sequins and thread for her embroidery. He would save the slippers until later. Aspasia's eyes sparkled with delight. She put the earrings on and looked at herself in the hand-mirror, moving her head from side to side to allow them to swing freely. The gold glinted in the lantern light. She kissed his cheek and thanked him.

When it came time to retire to bed, Aspasia helped Christophorus undress and washed his body with warm soapy water. It was a ritual she loved as her gentle touch guaranteed that she would be rewarded with his affections.

'And now,' he said, after she had dried him, 'I have something else for you. He sat her down on to the bed and pushed up her robe above her thighs. When he saw her smooth, naked legs, his heart raced. Aspasia also, quivered with excitement. Then he opened the box, took out the slippers, and carefully placed them on her feet. Aspasia put her hand to her mouth and gasped with happiness.

'They are truly the most beautiful slippers I've ever seen,' she said, standing up and taking several steps on the carpet. 'They are so soft that I cannot find the words to describe how beautiful they feel; like walking on air.' Her face suddenly became serious. 'Oh, Christophorus, is it a sin to be so happy? If so, then I ask for God's forgiveness.'

He pulled her back onto the bed, took her in his arms and made love; a lion devouring his gazelle.

CHAPTER 4

Aspasia's Sadness.

Christophorus had deliberately avoided mentioning the Archduke Ferdinand's assassination to Aspasia for fear of sullying the evening. Besides, he was still convinced it would all blow over. On his arrival in Uşak the following morning, his superior called him into his office. He had something he wanted to discuss with him. When Christophorus entered the room, he knew it wasn't just about carpets.

'You've heard, I presume,' Ferit Ali said, anxiously tapping a pen on a document in front of him.

'If you're talking about the incident in Sarajevo, yes.'

'Murky business, Christophorus, I fear this incident will open old wounds. If it does, it will be disastrous for the empire, but more importantly, it will be a disaster for our company. We rely on foreign investment.'

Christophorus reiterated what he had said to Nurettin. 'It will all blow over.'

Ferit Ali had been in the carpet business all his life, and it was largely through hard work and his wide network of contacts

29

that The Anatolian Carpet Manufacturers Ltd., situated in the Rue des Tienturerie in Uşak, had expanded into what it what it was today, one of the largest carpet trading companies in Turkey. Its catalogue boasted branches in Constantinople, Smyrna, Paris, London, Vienna, New York, Cairo, and Alexandria, and it was affiliated with The East India Company in Amritsar, and Persian companies in Tehran and Tabriz. Inside the thick catalogue were pages upon pages of photographs of the finest quality carpets one could buy. No size was too small or large to produce. Their list of satisfied customers included Kings and Queens, Kaisers and Tsars and their exquisite designs graced some of the finest palaces, hotels, and homes in the world.

'Unfortunately, I cannot share your optimism, Christophorus. This is not just a European affair, it is our affair too. Russia will be forced to take sides, and that will affect us as it raises the threat of the annexation of Constantinople, the Straits, and Eastern Anatolia. We are vulnerable, and the great powers will hover like vultures over us. They have vested interests in seeing the Ottoman Empire collapse. It is the way of politics. And we still have trouble with Greece. They are making noises concerning the restoration of confiscated property from the last war. We can well do without this added pressure.'

It was a while since Christophorus had seen Ferit Ali so anxious. Not since the outbreak of the Balkan Wars had he been like this.

'Surely the government will use great diplomacy to ensure we don't side with anyone.'

'From what I understand from my sources in Constantinople, our leaders have differing opinions about who they favour in the event of a war.'

'I have the utmost faith in them preserving the integrity of the empire,' Christophorus said, trying to shake Ferit Ali out of his sombre mood.'

'Let us hope so. I hear that Cemal Paşa has gone to France — something about the two dreadnoughts the government commissioned to be fitted out in England. Apparently there are some difficulties as they should have been finished by now. Cemal intends to find out from our diplomats in France just what is going on. Hopefully that will shed some light on France and England's frame of mind with regards to this diplomatic mess.'

There was little more to be said on the subject. Anything else was conjecture and served no real purpose. The discussion turned back to carpets and Christophorus's trip to Bursa. The sacks of carpet yarns and silks had arrived, and Ferit wanted to know whether the prices this year were still in their favour. He congratulated Christophorus on another excellent buying trip and suggested the yarns be distributed to the weavers immediately to build up their stock — just in case.

*

Aspasia, in the meantime, had her own worries. She had not menstruated for two months and today she noticed spots of blood on the bed-sheets. The thought that she might be pregnant had given her cause for further happiness, but she had deliberately kept this news from Christophorus for fear of the evil eye. It was far too soon to rejoice openly. Now she feared something was wrong and her happiness plummeted. By the time her mother-in-law called at the house for mid-morning coffee, she had severe abdominal cramps.

31

'Goodness, child, you look terrible. What on earth's wrong,' Marika Stavrides asked. 'Sit down and let me make you a coffee.' She looked at Aspasia's face again and quickly decided coffee was not the right thing to drink. 'I think mountain tea will be much better for you.'

She placed the pale yellow liquid in front of her and watched until she drank it all. 'Have you eaten?' she asked.

'I'm not hungry. Perhaps I ate something that disagreed with me. I will be fine soon.'

Her mother-in-law took one look at the carpet loom standing against the wall and could see by the design that Aspasia had not done any work that morning. The bird motifs were exactly as they were yesterday. Not a row further along.

'Maybe you should go to Uşak with Christophorus and see a doctor,' she said, thinking of her own daughter who had died suddenly from unknown causes. 'There's no-one here who can help you.'

There was someone but Aspasia was not inclined to discuss this with her. Kyria Stavrides was a good woman, but she would tell Christophorus, and that was the last thing she wanted. After a while Aspasia said she needed to lie down.

'Alright, but call me if you need anything. I am always here for you.'

Aspasia kissed her mother-in-law's hand and bid her farewell. As soon as she was alone she hurriedly picked up the sheets, scrubbed away the blood, and hung them out to dry in the garden. They would dry in no time in the hot afternoon sun, well before Christophorus returned.

By mid-afternoon, when most of the villagers were having a siesta, Aspasia picked up a light-weight shawl, threw it over her head and shoulders, and left the house to go to Pınarbaşı. The heat was unbearable and the cicadas deafening. On long hot days and well into the night they could barely sleep for their high-pitch sound. When she reached the meydan, she found both coffee houses doing a thriving trade. A caravan train carrying sacks of liquorice from Antalya to Smyrna had stopped to rest and the camel drivers were taking advantage of refreshments and the narghile before continuing their journey. At least forty camels now rested in the dusty meydan. Two young boys, orphans who worked for Ancient Yusuf, the hankeeper, ran backwards and forwards to the fountain filling huge bowls with water for the camels to drink. The heat only served to amplify the stench, forcing Aspasia to pull her shawl tightly across her face.

She picked up her step and crossed the meydan to Pınarbaşı where, thankfully, the foul smells were replaced by fragrant jasmine that trailed profusely over the stone walls in creamy white clouds, and orange blossom from the trees that lined the road. Pınarbaşı was almost a mirror image of Stavrodromi; identical in size with no more than forty houses. Its main feature was the mosque with a single pencil-slim minaret and which stood halfway along the main road, whereas Stavrodromi had the white-washed Church of the Virgin, which stood on the hillside. Both villages had several communal ovens and a small grocery which sold everything from foodstuffs, to pots and pans, leather slippers, birdcages, kerosene, and the odd ribbons and buttons. For anything finer, the villagers had to make the two hour trip to Uşak.

The Greek children of Stavrodromi all went to their own school to receive a rudimentary education, and then on to a larger school in Uşak for the remaining few years. Pınarbaşı had no school and the Turks received their education from the Imam at the mosque or in Uşak. As a consequence, most of the inhabitants of Pınarbaşı could neither read nor write. Aspasia's friend, Saniye, was one such person. So it didn't come as a surprise when she arrived at Saniye's house to find her, head and face covered, sitting in her garden under the shade of the mulberry tree dictating a letter to a scribe. With them was Saniye's mother-in-law, Ayşe Baci.

Saniye was delighted to see Aspasia, but shocked to see her so pale and evidently in pain. She took her inside and sat her down on the divan while her mother-in-law fetched a glass of water.

'How long have you been like this, Sister?' Saniye asked.

The two women were not related, but following the Turkish custom, Saniye always referred to her friend as sister. Aspasia saw it as a sign of affection.

'Since this morning. There were spots of blood on...' Aspasia stopped, realising that the scribe could possibly overhear through the open window.

'It's alright; he was just about to leave anyway.'

Saniye went outside, paid the man for his services and bid him farewell, telling him to call by again the following week.

'He's gone,' she said, poking a loose strand of dark hair under her red kerchief. 'There's just the three of us. Cemal is out on the plateau tending the goats, so you can speak freely. You were saying about the blood.'

'I saw the spots on the sheets this morning. The pains came later. At first they were small cramps but by mid-morning the pain was unbearable. I'm scared.'

'Does Christophorus know about the pregnancy?'

'Of course not. I haven't even told my mother-in-law. They would worry. You're the only one who knows,' Aspasia glanced at the old woman standing by her in her white headscarf and baggy floral pantaloons, 'and your mother-in-law.'

Saniye exchanged glances with the old woman. Ayşe Baci asked Aspasia to lie down on the divan in order to examine her. Aspasia did as she was told. She hitched up her skirt and opened her legs wide. The top of her thighs were covered in bright red blood. Saniye fetched a bowl of warm soapy water and a towel whilst her mother-in-law pressed on various parts of Aspasia's abdomen with her bony, henna-stained fingers. Every now and again, Aspasia cried out in pain.

The old woman shook her head and sighed heavily. Then she proceeded to wipe away the blood.

'I'm going to lose it, aren't I?' Aspasia said. 'Please God, don't let that happen.'

Her payers went unanswered. The blood could not be stemmed.

'My child, I fear you are not strong enough to carry it,' Ayşe replied, wiping away another trickle of blood.

Aspasia let out a cry. 'It's a sin to be so happy. That's what it is. I'm being punished.'

She started to sob.

Both women held her hands. They knew exactly what she was going through. Saniye had been married for three years and still not produced a child. Each time, her pregnancy ended in a miscarriage. The last was the worst. She had almost reached full term with less than a month to go when her contractions started. When the foetus arrived, it was so deformed no-one knew if it was a boy or a girl. She cried for weeks. Now her husband was saying she was cursed and would take another wife. Thankfully he was persuaded not to do so by his mother who loved Saniye like her own daughter.

'Please don't cry, Aspasia,' Saniye said. 'It's not meant to be. God is good. He will give you another. I will pray to my God for you as you pray to yours for me, but for the moment you must stay here. We will make something special to help you.'

Ayşe Baci took a jug of goat's milk, emptied some into a pan and brought it to the boil. Next she pulled away several handfuls of leaves from bunches of dried wild herbs that hung from a thin, frayed rope over the fireplace and started to crush them with a mortar and pestle. After adding a small handful of dried roots, she slowly poured the hot milk over the mixture and stirred vigorously until it was the consistency of thick cream and handed it to Aspasia to eat with a spoon.

'Eat it while it's hot. It will help you.'

Aspasia took one spoonful and screwed up her face. When every last drop had been eaten, she lay back down on the divan and tried to rest. At first the pain eased, but soon intensified. An hour later, she doubled over and the foetus fell away. It was all over.

Saniye comforted her distraught friend. 'I'm so sorry. God will give you another.'

By the time Aspasia came to leave, both the bleeding and the pains had stopped. Saniye offered to walk her to the meydan. Early evening was the time when the two villages came alive, and today was no exception. The pair headed down the street, arm in arm, passing a woman leading a cow by a rope to pasture further up the hill. All the villagers knew each other well and gossip travelled fast. Thankfully Aspasia could rely on Saniye's integrity. As they passed the mosque, a handful of men came out and hurriedly made their way towards the Coffee House of the Moon. At this time in the evening, seats in both coffee houses filled quickly and no-one wanted to miss out. When they reached the meydan, the camel train had already departed and the two boys were busily shovelling up camel dung and putting it on a pile to be used on the fires later. Their master made good money from the dung, and thus the boys were always guaranteed extra pocket money which would usually be spent on tobacco. A group of Greek women were sitting on the low stone platform around the fountain, talking to each other. Marika Stavrides was with them and she greeted Saniye with affection. She wanted to know what the pair had been up to.

'I went to have a look at Saniye's carpet,' Aspasia said, before she could pry further. 'It's exceptionally beautiful and as it will be ready to go to the warehouse in a few days, I didn't want to miss it. Christophorus says he already has a buyer for it. And then we played cards.'

Saniye had a reputation as a skilled weaver so the remark was not entirely unexpected.

'I will pay you a visit tomorrow,' Saniye whispered, as they embraced goodbye. 'And please, don't sit at the loom. You need rest.'

CHAPTER 5

Woven from the Heart.

The colour had still not returned to Aspasia's cheeks by the time Christophorus returned home and she purposely reddened them with the juice of a pomegranate to look healthier. The trick hadn't worked, for there was nothing she could do to hide the lack of sparkle in her eyes. When he saw her new slippers were still where she left them the night before, and that she had not touched her weaving either, he questioned her.

'My morning star, what ails you? This is not like you.'

'I fear I must have eaten something that disagreed with me,' she replied, and busied herself preparing his meal while he checked over the latest catalogue of designs from The Anatolian Carpet Manufacturers Ltd. She suggested eating in the garden as the weather was still warm and it would be cooler outside. Christophorus agreed. Aspasia lit the charcoal together with a few dried twigs in a small terracotta pot and fanned the flames until the coals were white hot. Then she threaded pieces of meat that had been marinating in olive oil, lemon, and herbs, onto skewers and placed them over the coals.

She watched him through the small window and felt a surge of sadness. She could not burden him with her miscarriage. That was unthinkable. He might think her cursed as Cemal thought Saniye. She would just have to be strong and as Saniye said, there would be another time.

By the time darkness fell, the food was ready. She hung lanterns from the trees and arranged soft cushions on a kilim under the loquat tree. Compared to most gardens in the village, theirs was quite large and well-cared for. Christophorus had planted a variety of roses, an apricot and a walnut tree when they got married. The fig and the loquat trees were already there. Like the other gardens in Stavrodromi, it had a high stone wall and was completely private. Occasionally they made love in the garden too. What a joy that was. Christophorus told her that to make love under the stars in a garden filled with the perfume of blossoms and accompanied by an orchestra of cicadas, was something they would remember long after their bodies lost their vitality. The finest of poets could not write anything more beautiful, he told her. Aspasia hoped that tonight would not be one of those nights.

Don't receive him in your bed tonight Saniye had warned her. You must heal.

Christophorus sat down to eat, but Aspasia could see he also wasn't himself. She wondered if he had taken on too much. He had so much responsibility for one so young. When they had finished the meal, she asked him what was on his mind. At first he said nothing, but when she declared that could only mean he was unhappy with her, he opened up.

'Ferit Ali called me into his office today.'

Aspasia waited.

'Something has happened that may affect us and he's worried. I assured him all would be fine. Have you heard about the assassination?'

Aspasia had no clue as to what he was talking about. That sort of news didn't usually make it as far as Stavrodromi.

'The Archduke Ferdinand and his wife were assassinated in Sarajevo a few days ago.'

She stared at him and then burst out laughing, relieved that it was nothing more serious.

'For a moment you frightened me. Who are these people and what does this have to do with us?'

'The Archduke was heir to the Hapsburg throne of Austria-Hungary.'

Aspasia saw the seriousness on his face. 'I still don't see what that has to do with us. Surely such a terrible thing so far away cannot be cause for you to be so downcast.'

'You don't understand,' he sighed.

'You are right. Sarajevo is a long way from Stavrodromi and we have little to do with the Hapsburgs.'

'It's the connections that matter, especially if this gets out of hand.'

'Christophorus, we don't know anyone in the region. We don't even have family in Greece, which is nearer. Anatolia is a long way from all this. I fail to see how this will affect us.'

'Until Ferit Ali pointed a few things out, I didn't really understand the problem myself. Perhaps I didn't want to.'

Christophorus started to tell her about the various alliances and age-old animosities in the region as if she were a child incapable of comprehending such things which annoyed her. He went to great pains to point out the Ottoman association with Germany and how Sultan Mehmed V had appointed the German, Liman von Sanders, as commander of the Ottoman First Army in December 1913, barely six months earlier.

'And I believe that the cabinet is divided on potential allies should war break out. Both Enver and Talat Pashas are pro-German, whilst I believe Cemal firmly believes only an Entente Power could stem Russian ambitions.'

'You keep talking about Germany. I thought you said the Archduke was Austrian?'

'Therein lies the problem. The Kaiser will stand by the Austrians. If he does, then Russia will enter the fray, and you know the trouble the empire has with them. I don't need to go into all that.'

'Won't they just execute the murderer and that's that?'

'My sentiments exactly — at first. The thing is, the Austrians are convinced Belgrade is behind this, and are pushing Serbia into some sort of ultimatum. As you know, the Tsar protects the Orthodox Christians in the region and he won't hesitate to go Serbia's aid. In fact, that would give him an excuse to meddle even more in the region.'

Aspasia mulled over his words. 'Christophorus, if anything happens, and at this point, I don't believe anything will as good sense is sure to prevail, won't we, as Orthodox Christians, be safe? I mean, the Ottomans protect us now and God forbid, should the Russian's invade, then they will look after us too.'

In the state of confusion she found herself in, Aspasia's thoughts immediately jumped to survival. Christophorus shook his head at the turn the conversation had taken.

'For the moment it's all conjecture. If this, if that! It does no-one any good, and I have enough on my plate with work. I must collect the finished carpets from Stavrodromi, Pınarbaşı and other villages by the end of the week so that they can be catalogued and shipped overseas to fulfil orders. Business has been brisk this year and Ferit Ali has promised a pay rise. If I can make enough, I aim to buy you a home in Uşak where you can be nearer to your family, and I to my work.'

He turned his attention to Aspasia's own carpet. That also was supposed to be completed, but she had several inches of the body and a border to finish. Even if she worked non-stop, she could not complete it. Christophorus suggested that his mother help her. Aspasia said she would ask Saniye.

When the time came for Aspasia to wash Christophorus's body, she was thankful that the combination of tiredness and the conversation had dampened his ardour. He fell asleep within minutes. She tidied up and went back outside for a while to lie on the rug and mull it all over. Her husband's anxiousness worried her. Earlier thoughts about the miscarriage now started to fade in light of all this. She lay back on the cushion looking up at the stars wondering exactly where this far-away assassination would lead them to. She crossed herself and prayed. The future suddenly seemed less rosy.

*

The following Friday morning, Aspasia heard the clip-clopping of hooves coming up the street. This time, Christophorus was accompanied by two men on mules, each one laden with sacks of yarn from The Anatolian Carpet Manufacturers Ltd. The men had come to collect her carpet in exchange for a few sacks of wool. Leaving the animals outside the house, they placed the sacks in the garden under the loquat tree while Aspasia prepared them something to eat. The bulk of the wool for the rest of the villagers had been brought by camels and deposited for distribution at the Greek school. The camels were now being fed and watered in the meydan by the same boys who tended the caravan train the day before, whilst the men sat in both coffee houses partaking in refreshments before distributing the wool and collecting the carpets.

Aspasia had just managed to complete her carpet in time and taken it off the loom that very morning. The discarded warp still lay scattered on the floor whilst she hastily finished the top and bottom into a beautiful fringe before the men arrived. The men commented on its beauty.

'I stand in awe of such a work of art. You are truly gifted, Kyria Aspasia,' one of them said. 'Christophorus is most blessed to have married such a skilled weaver.'

Aspasia blushed.

Their stomachs refreshed, Christophorus rolled up Aspasia's carpet, threw it over his shoulder and left with the men for the school, stopping on the way to collect his mother's carpet also. By the time they got there, the men from Stavrodromi and Pınarbaşı were already starting to arrive, each carrying their women's rolled-up carpet either on their backs, or if they were lucky enough, on a donkey. Their wives accompanied them, carrying gifts of food for the visitors; biscuits and baklava freshly baked that morning in the village oven, as well as cheese, honey, spoon-fruits, and whatever else they could muster up. Cemal and Saniye were amongst them. He had sent a small boy to tend the goats in his place that day.

In no time at all the school room resembled a carpet market.

Each family handed their carpet over for a thorough inspection and the details of the carpet were carefully noted; size, the type of design, quality of weaving, which included not only the knots per inch, but the beauty of the back as well. After meeting the required standards, Christophorus gave them a stamped and signed certificate on behalf of The Anatolian Carpet Manufacturers Ltd. Further classification would take place in Uşak. Without a doubt, all the carpets viewed that day were of high quality. Some of the designs had been produced in the same family for generations and the women knew them by heart. Others, like the Greek women, were trying out new ones which had been designed in the company studio in Uşak, in which case they brought along the squared paper design for the men to check. One thing was for sure, they were all woven from the heart and not just for the money.

The men then presented the certificate to another man who acted as a cashier and was responsible for paying them. The name of the weaver and family was noted in a large accounts book, and a sum of money commensurate with the quality of the carpet would be handed over together with a receipt. A signature was required, but as not everyone was able to write their name, a finger print or mark was accepted instead.

Although the carpet weaving was done by women to supplement their income, as a general rule it was the men who took charge of the finances. Christophorus was the only one who allowed his wife her own money for her work. His own father had done the same and it was natural for him. To him, Aspasia was his partner as well as his wife and he respected her as such. Sadly, he knew he was in the minority, especially in a small village.

Once the carpets were handed over and the money paid, that was not the end. Most of the families were given a sack of wool, which also had to be signed for. The wool was to be spun either for the warp and weft or for the pile, and would be picked up in a week's time to be dyed in the factory dye-houses in Uşak. The best wool for carpets was determined by the breed of sheep and usually came from the first clip, and thereafter from the area around the neck and shoulders. Christophorus was a master in wool grading and made sure every weaver working for the company had the best quality, which in turn brought a better return for everyone concerned. The fact that the women were given wool to spin was something Christophorus had organized for the two villages only. Most of the spinning was now done by machines in the factories, and it had created a huge uproar amongst the women who worked in the villages throughout Anatolia as they saw their livelihood diminish. Spinning provided the older women a chance to earn a little extra for their family and it was a job they could do whilst tending their animals. Christophorus's standing in the local community soared when he managed to still give them this work.

Not all the women could spin. It was mostly the older women who did this job whilst the younger preferred to weave. After pocketing Saniye's money, Cemal signed for two sacks of wool on behalf of his mother who chose to spin the wool for the warp and pile. Christophorus winced when he saw the way Cemal treated Saniye. She stood behind him, head bowed submissively; a mere shadow in his presence. He had heard of their problems and the fact that he wanted to take another wife, but there was little anyone could do.

After a few hours the business concluded and the weavers

departed. The day the carpets were picked up was always a day for celebration for both villages and the men headed to the coffee houses whilst tables were set up in the meydan and lambs roasted over the coals. By sunset the meydan would be filled with villagers dressed in their finery, dancing and eating.

By the time the celebrations were due to start, Aspasia felt much better and decided to accompany Christophorus and his mother to the meydan. The festivities gave her a chance to dress up in her traditional costume which she rarely wore these days. She pulled her hair back into a loose knot and wrapped her embroidered kerchief around her head letting it hang to a point which reached half-way down her back. Christophorus's filigree earrings from Bursa complimented the coins that jangled playfully from the edging of the kerchief perfectly.

Resplendent in her full costume comprising of a navy tunic embroidered in red silk, silver and gold gilt thread, belted at the waist with a narrow strip of fabric onto which was attached a large ornate silver buckle, Christophorus remarked on how beautiful she looked. She in turn, commented on how handsome he looked in his own outfit which consisted of a striped, woven tunic under which he wore a white shirt and trousers, a kerchief wrapped around his head from which hung a shoulder-length tassel at the side, and a highly polished pair of black boots. It made a change from his suit which made him look older and much more serious.

He gave her a kiss. How was it possible to be so fortunate, he thought to himself? Aspasia's own bliss was marred by the nagging thought that such happiness would be cursed.

The sun was setting by the time they reached the meydan and it seemed that everyone, old and young had gathered to join in the celebrations. A group of local musicians were playing lively traditional tunes and both coffee houses were doing a roaring trade. They had even employed several young boys for the evening to make sure the narghiles were constantly filled with water and replenished with bowls of fruit-scented tobacco. Christophorus spotted Cemal sitting outside the Coffee House of the Moon with a group of friends. He looked to be in high spirits. Saniye was by the fountain with her mother-in-law. Aspasia joined them while Christophorus settled himself at a long table in the middle of the meydan with the other men from Uşak. Tonight, they were guests of the villagers and as such, had prominent seating near the lamb roasting on the spits.

An old man and a teenage boy arrived with a dancing bear. The musicians stopped playing while the boy led the bear around the meydan by a chain, prodding and poking it with a stick to make it dance to the rhythm of the drums metered out by the man. When the boy was sure they had received an adequate amount of money, they sat near the camels to rest for a while and count their takings while the musicians resumed playing.

Aspasia thought Saniye unusually quiet. When the food was finally ready to be served, Saniye refused to eat.

'What's wrong?' Aspasia asked. 'Is it Cemal?'

Saniye nodded. 'He's finally done it,' she said, the tears streaking her beautiful moon-shaped face. 'He's found another wife. She will arrive tomorrow.'

CHAPTER 6

The Arrival of Fatma

Cemal's new bride was to be a twelve year old girl from a nearby village. Her father was a shepherd and unbeknown to Saniye, the marriage was arranged over several weeks on the plateau whilst both men were tending their animals. When he told his mother of the decision, she prostrated herself on the ground before him, pleading with him not to do it. Saniye had no say in the matter. She was outside in the garden feeding the chickens when she heard her mother-in-law wailing loudly. At first she thought someone had died and rushed inside to see what was wrong. The look on both their faces told her what was happening. Saniye took a step backwards and collapsed into a heap on the divan, sobbing uncontrollably.

'Who is this son I have given birth to?' Ayşe Baci cried, 'Only a fool cannot see what treasures he has before him. You have a good woman and look how you treat her.'

Cemal was getting angry. 'May your mouth be dried up, Mother. Does Allah not demand respect from a mother to her only son?'

Ayşe Baci feigned a spitting sound. 'The Almighty Allah will curse you for this.'

He pushed her aside with his foot and stormed out of the house to drown his sorrows. Their cries could be heard in the street as he cursed them for making his life a misery. The camels and mules carrying the carpets to Uşak had already left, but both coffee houses were still open serving a handful of regulars. Apart from that, the meydan was now empty. Hasan, the proprietor of the Coffee House of the Moon already knew about Cemal's intention to take another bride, and he could see by the sour look on his face it hadn't gone down well.

'*Hoş geldin*. Welcome, Cemal. What can I get you?'

'Bring me a bottle of raki.'

It was frowned upon in certain Muslim circles to drink, but in Pınarbaşı, those rules were often broken. Some said it was the Frankish influence that had made its way from Constantinople and Smyrna, but Hasan didn't complain as he made quite a substantial profit on alcohol. The only time they refrained was when Imam Süleyman was around, but by now he would be in his bed, snoring loudly on a full stomach.

'So they didn't take it too well then?' Hasan said, as he put the bottle and glass on the table.

'Bah,' growled Cemal. 'I get more sense from my goats!'

Hasan commiserated with him. It wasn't right that he didn't have a child after three years of marriage. A child was another mouth to feed, but at least in time it would contribute and look after him in old age. Cemal was a simple man and reasoning was not his strong point. He stayed in the coffee house steadily getting drunk until Hasan told him he must close or he would have marital problems himself. He didn't return home. Instead he spent the night on the plateau with his goats.

The following morning, he sent someone to the house for his good clothes to welcome his new bride. The bride arrived in Pınarbaşı riding a donkey decked out in coarse woven fabrics, tassels, and bells. She was covered from head to toe in a brightly coloured, red veil and matching tunic, under which she wore white pantaloons. Every now and again, one caught a glimpse of her ornate jewellery, which jangled noisily under her veil. Accompanying her were her parents and extended family. A handsome dowry consisting of six goats and two sheep, a wooden chest laden with kilims, a knotted carpet, embroideries and a few trinkets, were handed to the bridegroom in exchange for a cheap bracelet and a handful of coins for the young girl to sew on to her headdress. Cemal also guaranteed a sum of money for the girl should the marriage end in divorce.

In front of a small gathering, the marriage contract was signed, and an official well versed in the teachings of the Koran gave his blessings to the couple. A sheep had been offered up to God earlier that day and was now roasting on the spit where the villagers had congregated two nights earlier. Afterwards Cemal took his bride home. That night Saniye slept in the garden comforted by her mother-in-law.

*

Aspasia didn't see Saniye for a couple of days, but she did hear about Cemal's new bride. The whole village knew about it. Christophorus was appalled. He advised Aspasia to stay away, but she couldn't stop worrying. During the day, she took to

51

sitting by the fountain with her spindle in the hope that Saniye would appear, but she never did. In the end, she asked her mother-in-law to call at the house on the pretext of finding out if either Saniye or her mother-in-law needed help with the spinning.

Marika Stavrides waited until she knew Cemal would be on the plateau, then made her way to Pınarbaşı. Ayşe Baci answered the door. At first she looked frightened and almost closed the door in her friend's face.

'Good day, my friend. I come in peace and to see if you need any help with the spinning.'

The old woman indicated for her to come inside. The atmosphere was tense. A skinny, slip of a girl, who appeared to be no older than twelve years old, was in the kitchen trying to roll out sheets of yufka. When Saniye saw who the visitor was, she came over and kissed her hands. Marika was shocked to see her so pale and drawn. Ayşe Baci introduced the young girl as Fatma. Her dark eyes lowered, she bowed and offered to make the women tea.

'Christophorus tells me that someone will come to collect the yarn at the end of the week for dying. They have new orders, and if they cannot fulfil them in time, the traders will go elsewhere. I have told him we can't work any faster without compromising the quality.'

The three looked at the finished yarn, and it was evident Saniye was behind with her work, but no-one wanted to say anything about that in front of Fatma. Marika cast a careful eye towards the girl and decided to draw her into the conversation.

'Do you weave, my daughter?' she asked.

The girl shook her head. It was unusual that a girl her age could not weave carpets.

'Do you spin then?'

Again she shook her head.

'Well then, surely you must embroider?'

Fatma wrung her hands together nervously. 'Very badly, Kyria.'

The women all looked at each other.

'I am afraid she was of more use to her family tending sheep rather than learning a trade,' Ayşe said. 'She really can't do much at all.'

Marika Stavrides had come to the house because she felt sorry for Saniye. Now she felt sorry for them all. That miserable Cemal, she thought to herself. What a calamity he had brought on this household.

'Daughter, you need a skill. Do you want to learn?' she asked.

'Of course,' Fatma replied, 'if someone will teach me.'

Saniye turned away. She wanted nothing to do with her.

'Perhaps you could start by learning to spin. Come here, I will show you how easy it is.' Marika patted the cushion next to her and the girl sat down. Then she picked up Saniye's spindle and attached a piece of fleece to the hook. Next she gave the spindle a twist.

'Watch carefully. I lay the fleece over my left hand and as the spindle spins, I gradually guide the fleece with my other hand and it begins to twist into yarn.' She did it for a few minutes and then handed it to the girl. 'Now you have a go.'

At first, the girl was all fingers and thumbs, which made the women giggle, but after a while, she began to get the hang of it.

'There you are,' Marika smiled, patting the girl's thigh. 'Everyone can learn a skill. When you have mastered that, I am sure Ayşe Baci will teach you how to knot carpets, won't you, my friend?'

Ayşe's cheeks reddened and the smile dropped from Saniye's face. Just what did Kyria Stavrides mean by interfering like this? After the women had finished their tea, Marika bid her hosts farewell.

'I don't understand, Kyria Marika,' whispered Ayşe, when they were out of earshot of Saniye and Fatma. 'It's not like you to come here and cause trouble'.

'That is not my intention, my dear friend. Aspasia has a plan to get Saniye out of her misery. Christophorus told us that the company has orders for larger carpets and they will pay well. Aspasia said she would like to try her hand at them and she wants Saniye to weave with her. Of course she will need a bigger loom, but that's not a problem. Don't you see, Ayşe, if you help Fatma, Cemal will be happy and leave Saniye to weave as she pleases. You will all win. Saniye will be out of the house for much of the time, the girl will learn a trade and be a useful contributor, and your son will be happy because he will have a contented household and double the income.'

Ayşe smiled. 'You are a crafty one, Kyria Marika, you and your daughter-in-law. I thank God you are my friend. Go home and tell Aspasia, it will be as you wish. I give you my word.'

CHAPTER 7

A Carpet fit for a King.

After seeing off a camel train laden with 50 bales of carpets for the warehouse in Smyrna, Christophorus tidied up his paperwork in readiness to go home. The last few weeks had been exceptionally busy, and although the company had made a lot of money, Ferit Ali's nervousness at the likelihood of a full-scale war was catching. In the end, his fears came to fruition. Austria-Hungary declared war on Serbia on the 28th of July, and Germany joined their ally as predicted. After the Germans invaded Belgium, France and Britain mobilized. Even worse, Germany declared war on their unpredictable enemy, Russia. It seemed that almost everyone was at war except the Ottoman Empire. For the first time in his life, Christophorus felt scared. Ferit Ali showed him the telegraphs that were coming through on a daily basis. The foreign warehouses needed to be stocked and the carpets had to leave Turkey as soon as possible before something disastrous happened.

In Stavrodromi and Pınarbaşı, the yarn had been collected and dyed and the weavers were all knotting again. They had all been promised extra money if they could finish earlier, but there is only so much a weaver could do. On average, 8,000 — 9,000 knots per day was the amount a skilled weaver could produce. Any more was generally considered to be unsustainable and the quality was likely to suffer. Most of the village weavers only produced half that amount.

Christophorus called into the design studio, a small building attached next to the factory, before returning home. He was to pick up the new design for Aspasia and Saniye. At the moment the larger loom had been set up in the garden and the women were eager to try it out.

'How do you like it, Kyrios Stavrides?' Sara, the designer asked. 'I tried my best to replicate the photo.'

Christophorus compared the picture to the drawing. It was a replica of a 17th century Uşak star carpet of exceptional beauty, and similar to a pair that had been made in the workshops for King Edward VII of England a few years earlier. A photograph of the Turkish Ambassador presenting the King and Queen with the gift on behalf of Sultan Abdülhamit shortly before he was deposed by the Young Turks in 1909, hung on Christophorus's wall in his office as a reminder of The Anatolian Carpet Manufacturers Ltd.'s standing in the industry. Large floating blue star-shaped medallions and half-medallions filled the red ground and between them, scattered throughout the field were small geometric flowers joined together by a thin tracery of stem-work. The body of the carpet was surrounded by a border consisting of two narrow bands and a larger central one.

The design was painted on squared paper with each square representing a knot. The designer, who knew Aspasia from the days when she worked in the factory, was aware of her skills, so had only painted a section of the repeat as she was sure she would be able to work the rest out for herself.

'Magnificent, Sara,' Christophorus exclaimed. 'Simply, wonderful. Your design work is excellent.'

Even on first glance, he knew this carpet would fetch a tidy sum when completed. Such carpets as these were in high demand. A good one was rare, and the right buyer would pay handsomely, enough to buy them the longed-for new house in Uşak. When Aspasia suggested working on a large carpet with Saniye, Christophorus was sceptical at first, but soon saw there was merit in it, and he liked the idea of her working with Saniye. It would give her the chance to be with someone her own age. More importantly, Saniye was an excellent weaver.

Sara attached the design to a stiff board to prevent the edges being ripped during use, and wrapped it in paper, then in a cloth. She had also calculated how much yarn would be needed and had prepared the skeins for him in a large sack. Two blues, two reds, an apricot, dark green, saffron, and ivory.

'There's more of the rich red and darker blue,' she told him. 'And just in case she runs out, I have put some aside from the same dye batch.'

Christophorus gave her a handful of coins for her trouble, but Sara refused to take it. She and Aspasia had grown up together, and she regarded her as a good friend.

Returning to his office, he spotted Ferit Ali running across the yard towards him waving a telegram.

'What did I tell you, Christophorus? I knew it! The government has issued orders to close the Dardanelles. We are finished, I tell you, finished!'

Ferit Ali's body shook like a leaf. Christophorus suggested

they go to the bar in the Hotel Europa where the carpet merchants stayed, to gather their thoughts. It was only a few streets away, but Ferat Ali sobbed all the way there. They also saw several men nailing notices on the walls, calling for men to mobilize.

The place was bustling with carpet dealers and foreign journalists.

'Two large whiskeys,' Christophorus said to the bartender.

Two of their French and English traders came over to join them.

'A sad day,' the Englishman said, 'but not entirely unexpected when the government signs a secret deal with the Germans. If you ask me, the Ottomans should not have done this.'

Christophorus had no idea what they were talking about. He knew nothing of a secret deal. That was a world away from his life.

Fueled by drink, Ferit Ali argued that they had no choice.

'By allowing the SMS *Goeben* into Ottoman waters first, and then closing the Straits, surely that's sending a message that you are siding with the Germans.'

'The British government requisitioned our dreadnoughts. They had no right to do that. They were paid for by the Turkish people. We scrimped and saved for those ships. Even school children gave their money. It's a disgrace.'

The English trader backed off.

Christophorus was afraid Ferit Ali would do something silly if he kept drinking and pulled him aside. 'Let's eat,' he said. 'The hotel has a fine menu and the tables are filling fast.'

'You have to get home,' Ferit Ali replied, when he had calmed down. 'Your wife will worry about you.'

'And yours will worry about you if you carry on like this.'

Christophorus never spoke out of turn to his boss, but tonight his own nerves were frayed. They went into the dining room where an orchestra was playing a waltz. He looked around the room with its Belle Époque furniture, fine carpets and potted palms, whilst waiters served champagne and fine wines. Everything seemed the same. Women wore the latest Parisian fashions, their long pearls adorning their graceful necks, and men smoked cigars. It all seemed surreal. Only the journalists, lined up at the desk sending and receiving telegrams, appeared to be nervous. It was incomprehensible that events could have turned out like this. Surely sanity would prevail, even at this late stage. Tomorrow he would wake up and it would all be a dream.

*

Tired and dejected, Christophorus arrived home in the early hours of the morning. Aspasia was waiting up for him. She was beginning to feel much better after the miscarriage and had made a special effort to look attractive for him by perfuming her hair with rose oil and wearing her new slippers. One look at his face and she knew something was wrong again. It was getting to be a regular occurrence. Even the sight of her looking so beautiful failed to arouse him. Exhausted, he lay on the bed, fully clothed, and slept like a baby.

It was mid morning when he woke up. Aspasia was at the table still in her nightdress, studying the new carpet design. Skeins of wool lay in neat piles around her. By her calculations, it would take them a few months, even with the two of them working on it; much longer than her other carpets.

Christophorus rubbed his eyes and tried to focus. When she saw him stir, she went to make him a drink.

'It's wonderful,' she said, stirring the coffee in the briki. 'Possibly the best design Sara has ever done. It reminds me of the ones the factory made for the King of England. I hope we can do it justice.'

'It's almost the same,' Christophorus replied, 'just a few minor differences, mainly in the ground. If anything, yours is closer to the 17th century original, which I think is better.'

At the mention of the King of England, Christophorus thought of Ferit Ali and the English trader.

'I was so happy when I saw the design,' he said, ' and I couldn't wait to show you, but then Ferit Ali hit me with the news that the Ottomans have put mines at the entrance to the Dardanelles.'

Aspasia almost spilt the coffee.

'My God, Christophorus. Are we at war?'

'No, my darling, we are not.'

She brought over his coffee, put it by the side of the bed and cuddled up against him.

'I don't understand,' she said in a soft voice that reminded him of a child.

'Neither do I my love, but I might have to start spending a little more time in Uşak, just till things blow over. I will stay at the Hotel Europa. The company keeps several rooms available for clients.'

Aspasia nodded miserably. She looked so vulnerable. Christophorus lifted her chin towards him with his forefinger, looked into her eyes, and kissed her soft lips.

'And I promise to try and come back home at least once a

week at the very least. Do you think you will be alright on your own?'

Her eyes were moist with tears. 'Of course. I am quite safe here.'

Christophorus held her in his arms and stroked her hair, perfumed with rose oil. He noticed that she was wearing her cream slippers.

'How well they suit you, my morning star.'

'I shall wear them all the time if you are going to be away. They will remind me of you.'

She pulled her nightdress up to knees, twirled her feet and giggled playfully. When she placed a foot on his knee, he could not restrain himself. The tiredness of the night before was gone, and they made love. Outside the sun was shining, the birds were chirping and the aroma of fresh bread from a nearby communal oven filled the air. Another perfect Anatolian day.

CHAPTER 8

The Day the Birds Stopped Singing

The weeks passed as Aspasia and Saniye's carpet grew inch by inch, day by day. By the beginning of October, they had completed a third of it. Word soon spread through Stavrodromi and Pınarbaşı about its beauty, and the other weavers came to look saying they would also like to try something new. The thought that they would get extra money was also attractive. Each weekend, Christophorus came home as promised and was delighted with the women's progress. He also managed to move the loom into the house by the time the autumn winds chilled the air so that the girls could work more comfortably. Aspasia was in high spirits, and this pleased Christophorus enormously as it distracted him from the deepening crisis in the empire, which was worsening by the day, if not by the hour. However, he resolved not to bring his troubles home and managed to perfect an outgoing air of happiness for the sake of Aspasia and his mother. As such, the pair spent their weekends in marital bliss.

Whenever the skeins needed winding into balls, Aspasia and Saniye took to walking the two kilometre climb to the top of the hill to sit on the low wall that surrounded the Greek Church. From this vantage point they had a glorious view of the two villages below and across the wheat fields to the mountains beyond the plateau. On such days, Marika Stavrides and Ayşe Baci took it in turns to make them food. If it was Marika, she made either lamb koftes or tiropitakia, cheese triangles. If it was Ayşe Baci, she made stuffed aubergines or carrot rolls. It was always accompanied by either cherry or apricot juice. The two women never went hungry. Such days were filled with happiness and light-hearted chatter and their friendship grew even deeper.

One particular day in October, they finished unwinding their first two skeins and decided to eat. Aspasia unwrapped the cloth and laid out the food. Since they had been working together, Saniye had hardly mentioned Fatma, or Cemal for that matter. Today was different and Saniye sensed her friend wanted to talk.

'Fatma is with child,' Saniye said, tearing at a piece of bread and scooping up a broken piece of kofte.'

They had both dreaded this moment. Now it was a reality and neither could bring themselves to accept it.

'Are you sure?' said Aspasia. 'What I mean is, they haven't been married very long.'

Saniye laughed. 'It only takes one moment of passion. Some people are lucky that way.'

Aspasia let her friend talk.

'She has morning sickness. What makes it worse is that Cemal makes us wait on her hand and foot. "Fatma is not allowed to sit at the loom. Fatma must not stand in the kitchen and make yufka. Fatma must not be allowed to fetch water from the fountain," and on and on. We carry her burden, and get no thanks for it. And he has not touched me since she came to the house. I have a good mind to see Imam Süleyman and ask for a divorce on the grounds of cruelty.'

Aspasia could see Saniye was not joking.

'What would you do? Where would you go?' Aspasia asked. 'Would he even divorce you?'

Aspasia knew that Cemal saw Saniye as someone who brings in the money because of her weaving and he would never let her go. Her friend was in an unhappy marriage and there seemed no way out. Worse still, she loved him, although for the life of her, Aspasia couldn't understand why. Cemal was a morose little man, prone to outbursts of violence if he didn't get his own way. He was an only child, and Ayşe Baci had spoilt him, especially after the death of his father. Some said that death was a result of a feud on the plateau about a stolen goat or sheep. The story was vague and Cemal seemed destined to bear the guilt of the father's sins.

'There's something else,' Saniye said. 'I didn't want to tell you before but I have problems with my brother, Mehmet, in Constantinople. You remember when you came to the house and the scribe was there? Well, he's been to the house a few times. Mehmet is asking for money.'

Aspasia was shocked. Saniye and Cemal were not wealthy.

'He never found a good job after he came back from Thrace, so he decided to stay on as an army reservist. It gave him food and shelter. At first he wanted money because he found a girl he wanted to marry. I said I couldn't help him. He told me to ask Cemal to sell one of his goats.' Saniye laughed. 'Can you imagine that? He loves his animals more than us.'

Aspasia asked why Saniye didn't say something earlier. Perhaps Christophorus could have helped.

'Mehmet is persistent. He wrote again, but it was about the time Fatma came to live with us. After that, it was impossible to discuss it with Cemal.'

'So what did you do?' Aspasia asked. 'Didn't you have any money at all left from the sale of your carpets?'

'I never saw that money. Cemal pocketed it all. In the end I decided to send him some of my jewellery; a bracelet and necklace that was part of my dowry. It was worth quite a bit and I knew Cemal would never notice.'

'And has he stopped pestering you now?'

'That's just it. He's asking for more.'

Aspasia was appalled. 'Can't he find a job at all? Perhaps Christophorus can find him a job in one of the warehouses.'

Saniye sighed heavily. 'It's more serious than that I'm afraid.'

'What on earth do you mean? Is he ill?'

On seeing her friend's reaction, Saniye deliberated over what to say.

'Hasn't Christophorus said anything to you?'

'About what?'

'The government is mobilizing for war and they are calling the men up. The reservists were the first to be called. The only way they can get out of it is to pay an exemption fee, and I don't have any more to send him. Mehmet was lucky to return from Thrace, but if he goes to fight again, he may never return.'

Aspasia felt an acute tightening in her chest and her head started to throb. It was as though everything was frozen in time. Then she noticed something odd. The birdsong that had accompanied them over the past few hours had stopped. Even the light breeze that rustled through the grass had dropped. An eerie silence surrounded her — except for the dull thudding of her heart pounding in her chest. Her eyes fell on an old widow clad from head to toe in black approaching the church. She had come to pour oil over the bones of her loved ones at the ossuary nearby. Deep in prayer, the woman ignored them. Aspasia crossed herself and prayed.

Saniye could see the look of fear in Aspasia's eyes.

'I'm sorry, Sister. I didn't mean to burden you with my worries. Whatever is going on can't possibly affect us here. We must be thankful that we are far away from these problems.'

CHAPTER 9

The Drums of War

In Uşak, Christophorus now spent more of his time at the Hotel Europa than he did at the factory. The feverish boom of the first half of 1914 had been snuffed out with lightening speed. The women were still weaving, but the carpets were stockpiling in the warehouses and the orders virtually ground to a standstill.

Ferit Ali went to Smyrna to see if he could drum up more trade and left Christophorus in charge. Most of the carpet industry was in the hands of foreigners who had enjoyed tax exemptions for years. In a remarkable turn of events, the Porte abolished the "capitulations" during the first week of October. Thousands of Levantines who were also Ottoman citizens, and who had enjoyed a special status since Byzantine times were now forced to give their full allegiance to the Ottoman State or face deportation. This also meant that they were now faced with hefty tax bills to help the war effort. Most of the banking and commerce was in the hands of the Greeks, Armenians, Jews and Levantines, and this latest news sent shock waves through the empire. Everyone started to plan for the worst.

Their fears were realized. The government began calling up not only reservists like Mehmet, but citizens too. And it wasn't only the Muslims in the empire. This time the Christians were ordered to report for duty as well. Throughout the weeks, Uşak saw many more of its menfolk leave for the military and no-one seemed to know where they were going or what would happen. They had been mobilizing for two months now, but it wasn't easy for Christophorus to gauge the full extent of the situation as stories conflicted. All he knew was that not everyone in the Sublime Porte saw eye to eye. In his naivety, he kept thinking it was a temporary situation and they would return.

Over dinner one evening, one of the reporters at the Hotel Europa told him that a shipment of one million pounds in gold had arrived at Constantinople's Sirkeci station from Germany. Now Christophorus was sure the Ottomans would side with the belligerents. Little wonder their customers were deserting them in droves. Another shipment of gold arrived soon after and then on the 19th October, the Ottoman Empire launched a surprise attack on the Russian Fleet in the Black Sea and the coastal ports. By the end of the month, the British Government wired all ships in His Majesty's Service, especially those in the Mediterranean, to prepare for war against Turkey. As predicted, Tsar Nicholas was quick to inform his subjects that Russia was at war with its old enemy, Turkey, "that ancient oppressor of the Christian faith and of all the Slavic nations."

The unthinkable had finally happened. Ottoman Turkey was now at war. The night the news was finally delivered to him, Christophorus drank so much whisky he had to be carried to bed. The thought that he could no longer put off telling Aspasia sickened him to the core. Ferit Ali arrived back from

Smyrna in tears. He told Christophorus that he had cried more in the past few days than in the whole of his lifetime, and if this went on much longer his weak heart would fail him.

After a while, he pulled himself together. 'We must try and carry on regardless,' he said. 'Sooner or later the stockpiled carpets will be back on the market again and we must be well prepared.'

He also reminded Christophorus that as yet, America was not at war, and they did a lot of business there. That at least gave him some encouragement.

'And where do we get the money to pay the workers?' asked Christophorus.

Ferit Ali told him to follow him into his private room next to his office.

'Shut the door,' he said. 'This is for your eyes only.'

He pulled a small chest of drawers away from the wall revealing a hidden metal door. Taking a small key from his pocket, he unlocked it and pulled out a large box. In it were hundreds of thousands of bank notes in various currencies, and a bundle of papers of stock holdings and bonds. Christophorus's mouth dropped open. He knew Ferit Ali secreted money around the place, but this amount of money shocked him. He was speechless.

'I brought some more back with me from Smyrna,' said Ferit Ali. 'Some of our foreign traders had a meeting and decided to entrust it to me to carry on until things revert back to normal. I cannot carry this burden alone. What if something happens to me?' He patted his heart. 'You never know. That is why I now entrust it to you, should something unforeseen happen.'

Christophorus pulled out a chair and sat down, mopping the sweat from his brow.

'Good Lord, man, if the government finds out about this we are done for,' he replied.

'We must look after our business, Christophorus. The government only cares about itself.'

He took out a wad of notes, pushed the box back in the wall and locked the door.

'Here, this key is for you. Keep it somewhere safe. I have another.'

Ferit Ali started to count the money. 'It is now common knowledge that the Christians are being called up too and unfortunately you are in that age group. Thankfully, I am too old. The thing is, the company cannot do without you. More importantly, you are a friend and I cannot do without you. Therefore, I am giving you this money to pay your exemption fee, plus I will write a letter to the authorities telling them that you are a vital employee of The Anatolian Carpet Manufacturers Ltd., and should the need arise, will be in a position best served to help the war effort here in the factory rather than the military.'

Christophorus was aware that the Ottoman Christians were being conscripted and so far had managed to avoid it, but he knew his time was running out. In previous wars, the Christians were deemed too much of a risk to arm and recruit, so if the Porte had changed tactics, then this must be serious, and he knew it would only be a matter of time before he, too, was called up. He was also aware of the exemption fee and unbeknown to Aspasia, had put some money aside. If Ferit Ali was offering to pay this for him, then he would give Aspasia his own money. It occurred to him that everyone was hiding what they could, and the authorities would be mindful of that fact.

Ferit Ali put the money in a paper bag and handed it to him.

'Don't forget, there's more in the box should you need it.'

Christophorus tucked the package in his inside jacket pocket.'

'And don't lose that key,' Ferit Ali said with a smile. 'Now, let's go and drown our sorrows at the Europa.'

Outside the factory, they were met with the rhythmic music of drums and pipes. The musicians were parading up and down the main street of Uşak attracting quite a crowd. This time several recruiting officers were with them espousing the benefits of joining up, not least of which was the immense moral pressure, and the gratitude of the Sultan in the cause of preserving the empire. It wasn't as if they had any choice anyway. Failure to report for duty when you were of fighting age meant imprisonment.

Christophorus and Ferit Ali picked up their step. One of the recruiting officers, Abdullah, son of a small-time shopkeeper, knew them and called out.

'Sons of the empire, we hope you will do you your duty.'

The Hotel Europa's lobby was filled with suitcases and the place was swarming with people of every persuasion, all frantically deciding what to do next. Businessmen from the east on their way to Constantinople or Smyrna were in a dilemma. The banks had put a moratorium on drawing out money, and trade had all but come to a standstill. Apart from the usual businessmen and journalists, a new class of people now made their presence known — the Military. Sotiris Lambros, the Greek proprietor of the hotel pulled Ferit Ali aside.

'I am at my wit's end,' he said, his forehead lined with stress. 'The Military are demanding rooms and my best customers are leaving. This is disastrous.'

'It's disastrous for us all, Kyrios Lambros,' Ferit Ali replied. 'Let's hope we can pull through.'

The dining room was full and they were about to walk away when one of the English carpet traders called them over and made room for them at their table.

'Ferit Ali Efendi, Kyrios Stavrides, please join us. I fear this will be the last night we will enjoy your company. We are now enemies and as such have forty-eight hours to leave.' He looked around the room. The orchestra was playing a tango but the dance floor was empty. 'You will have all this to yourselves tomorrow evening.'

The mood had changed dramatically. Gone was the usual lively atmosphere. Christophorus counted only two women. The rest had either left or were in the process of packing their jewels and fine clothes.

'What can I say, my friends?' Ferit Ali said, shrugging his shoulders.

There was little to say.

The following morning, Christophorus looked outside his bedroom window as he dressed. Porters were busy taking suitcases and rolls of carpets to the train station and people were shaking hands, saying their goodbyes. The drums had started up again and were parading up and down the main street. By the time he reached the breakfast room, most of the foreign guests had already left. The waiter brought him breakfast, but he felt too sick to eat. He took a few sips of his coffee and left.

Ferit Ali gave him a few days leave, but before he went home to Stavrodromi there were a few things he needed to do. The first was to pay a call at the recruitment centre. Men stood in long lines patiently waiting their turn to sign up. Several officials were still booming out the benefits of joining up, but he could see by the looks on their faces, most did not believe it. Even worse, the lines were also filled with Greeks and Armenians, husbands and brothers of most of the workers in the factories. He knew most of them, and felt a terrible sense of guilt as he walked past them to another, smaller line for those paying exemption fees. The guilt weighed heavily on his mind.

When he was shown into the office, he came face to face with the same official he had encountered the night before when he was going to the Hotel Europa with Ferit Ali.

'So, Kyrios Stavrides, what can I do for you?'

'Forty-three pounds, I believe, Abdullah Efendi,' Christophorus said, as he placed Ferit Ali's letter on the desk along with an envelope containing the exorbitant exemption fee.

The official counted it. There was another twenty pounds extra for himself which he pocketed without saying a word. A vast amount for an official and he knew it. He read the letter and smiled.

'Your company is well placed to help us out, Kyrios Stavrides. We will be in need of wool for blankets and clothing for the army. The snow is already falling in the border provinces.'

Christophorus's heart sank. 'We will do whatever we can, Efendim, my sir. You can rely on The Anatolian Carpet Manufacturers Ltd.'

'I am sure we can,' Abdullah replied, with more than a hint of sarcasm. 'Especially now that your foreign business associates have either deserted you or taken out full Turkish citizenship, which means that your company will now be paying more tax. That alone will help the war effort.'

Christophorus knew the official was being deliberately

provocative, but there was little he could do. He didn't like the man, and was well aware that this small-time official was typical of many who would use the war as an excuse to further their position. He already had an office of his own, and most likely more money than he had seen in his lifetime stuffed in his pockets. He was well on the devious road to success.

CHAPTER 10

The Village of Disillusionment

Even before Christophorus reached Stavrodromi, he knew something was wrong. The last kilometre of road snaked down from the plateau to the village through a narrow valley of scrub and myrtle bushes used by shepherds and goatherds on their way to greener pastures. Often he would see one or two of the villagers in the distance. Occasionally it was the Greek shepherd, Ilyias, owner of a ferocious looking Anatolian sheepdog with its spiked collar worn to defend himself in fights against wolves attempting to feast on the lambs. More often than not, it was Cemal. Today, the men were nowhere in sight. Then he noticed Ayşe Baci sitting on a rock. When she saw him, she waved frantically and scrambled down the rocky pathway towards him. Christophorus didn't need to be told what was wrong. Seeing her tending the goats instead of Cemal told him that not even the men of Stavrodromi and Pınarbaşı had been able to avoid mobilization.

'They took him,' Ayşe Baci cried, tears streaking her face.

Christophorus dismounted his horse as the distraught

woman prostrated herself in front of him alternately beating her fists on the earth and then throwing her arms up towards the sky.

'Kyrios Christophorus, I beg you, please help us.'

He pulled her up and held her in his arms. Her body shook with emotion.

'Aspasia, Saniye,' he asked. 'Tell me, are they alright?'

Thanks be to Almighty Allah, yes. But it is we women who are left to suffer, not knowing if we will ever see our menfolk again.'

Christophorus had a good idea of which men would have left. All the same, he asked.

'Ten,' replied Ayşe Baci. 'Sons, brothers and fathers.'

She started wailing again.

'Calm down, please. This won't do any good. I will do what I can but for the moment I must get home.'

He wrenched himself from her grip and jumped back on his horse. It was midday, when he entered the meydan, the time when there should have been quite a few people going about their daily business. Today, it was empty. The clip-clopping of his horse's hooves clattered loudly in the silence. He made his way to the han where Ancient Yusuf was sitting on the floor asleep, his back propped up against a large piece of carved stone that had fallen down from the ornately curved portal longer than anyone could remember. He was snoring loudly, oblivious to the fact that Christophorus had arrived.

Christophorus kicked him lightly on his foot. 'Hey, Yusuf, you white-bearded old goat, get up and do some work. My horse needs a good feed.'

Yusuf rubbed his eyes. When he saw who it was, he jumped

up immediately, took the horse's bridle and stroked the mare's black mane. Having been born in the han, she was a friendly horse and well used to Yusuf now. She flicked her tail and nuzzled her head into his chest.

'Thanks be to Allah you are safe,' he said. 'How did you manage to evade them?'

Christophorus was wary about mentioning the exemption fee in case the villagers turned against him.

'The factory will be producing goods for the government, so my services are required there.'

He followed Yusuf into the han as he led his horse to a stall reserved especially for him, took off the bridle and saddle, and hung it on a large hook. Nearby, several other horses and donkeys were tethered in the stalls. Christophorus knew full well some of them belonged to men who had now joined up.

'I hope the men return soon because if they don't, I won't be able to feed them,' Yusuf said.

He gave a shrill whistle and the two boys appeared.

'Fetch some food for the horse,' Yusuf ordered. 'And water.'

One of them placed a bundle of hay in the horse's stall along with a few bowlfuls of grain and watched it eat whilst the other ran outside to fetch water.

'Thank God I am too old to fight. I've seen enough fighting to last me a few lifetimes,' Yusuf said with a heavy sigh. 'Only Allah the Almighty knows what is in store for those poor souls.'

Christophorus gave him a few coins and one each to the two boys and told him he would be staying a couple of days at least. Then he made his way home, passing the two coffee houses which were both closed. He couldn't recall the last time either of them closed. The village had few people, but it did have a thousand eyes, and Aspasia had got wind of his arrival. When he turned into his street, she was running to greet him.

'Oh my beloved, you are safe,' she said, 'throwing her arms around him. 'We have been frantic not knowing whether or not you had joined up.'

His mother was waiting in the doorway. She took her son's hands and kissed them.

'My son, my precious son, I was convinced they had called you up.'

Inside the home, the two women fussed over him with food and drink. Aspasia laid out fresh clean clothes, and after he had changed, they sat on the divan firing a barrage of questions at him. When he had put their minds at rest that he was not going to war, at least for the moment, they relaxed.

'Tell me,' he said, 'Who has been called up?'

The women went through a list of names. Nikos, Ilyias and Mikis. They were all shepherds.

'What about Tassos's son, Thanassos?' Christophorus asked, 'And Markos, Vassilis the grocer's son?'

Thanassos ran the Sun Coffee House for his father. His son was the same age as Cemal, twenty-nine. Markos was two years older.

'Tassos and Vassilis went to Uşak to pay an exemption fee for them. I'm surprised you didn't see them,' Aspasia said.

'Uşak is in turmoil at the moment,' Christophorus replied. 'No-one knows what's going on. And the Turks? Which of those left?'

Aspasia continued. 'Ömer, the Turkish grocer's son. What a scene that was. He begged his father to pay the exemption fee, but the old goat told everyone he couldn't afford it. I heard that

Hasan Efendi offered to help him out, but he still wouldn't hear of it.'

'Stubborn as a mule that one.' Marika Stavrides added. 'Now his son may die because of his vanity.'

Aspasia told him of four others including Cemal. 'I haven't seen Saniye for two days. She refuses to leave the house.'

The two women told them how Bekçi Baba, the man assigned to go round the villages and report the news appeared one day. He stood in the meydan beating his drum and calling out "men born between the years 1880 and 1885 are to report to the nearest recruiting centre or risk imprisonment."

'They were told they had forty-eight hours,' Marika continued. 'Then he went through both villages just to make sure we all heard. It was terrifying. Most of the men left the following day. The women are inconsolable. The Greek women spend their time at the church, and the Turkish at the mosque, unless they are like Ayşe Baci and look after the goats and Fatma's two sheep. Some officials came to the village to put up posters and answer any questions. Did you see the posters?'

Christophorus shook his head.

'They're in Greek and Turkish so the authorities are making sure we Greeks get the message also. They plastered one on the doors of both coffee houses, the school, and outside the mosque and church. There are also some on the trees in the meydan. I can't imagine how you missed them,' Aspasia added.

Marika Stavrides placed a plate of fried vegetables in front of him and cut him a thick slice of bread, freshly baked that morning.

Christophorus ate his meal in silence with both women sitting next to him, waiting for him to finish so that they could ask more questions.

'Pour me some wine,' he said to Aspasia.

She did as she was told. He downed the first glass in one gulp and she poured him another.

After he had mopped up the last drop of oil from his plate, His mother was the first to speak.

'This is the first time they have called the Christians up, my son,' she said, making the sign of the cross over her chest. 'I have a bad feeling in the pit of my stomach.'

She rubbed her abdomen in small circles to stress the point

'And this is the first time there has been a war like this,' Christophorus replied. 'They can hardly leave us out. The war will be fought on all fronts. That means they need us all.'

'Where will these men be sent to?' Aspasia asked.

'Who knows? The Aegean coastline, in case the enemy attacks there, the Russian front in the Caucasus, Iraq, and Egypt as the British have a foot in that area too.'

Aspasia started to cry. 'You're frightening me. They are border regions.'

Christophorus knew he could no longer protect the two women he loved the most from the truth.

'My dearest Aspasia, everything is being thrown into the war effort. The Porte cannot afford to lose this struggle. We are all praying that it will be over by Christmas, but if it's not, we have to face facts. More men will be called up and many will die. For those left behind, life will be hard. Who will be the breadwinner when the man is at war? Where will the money to live come from? The army will requisition everything. Foodstuff, kerosene, clothing; they've already told us that The Anatolian Carpet Manufacturers Ltd. will have to produce items for the army and you can be sure they are not talking about carpets.'

He looked at Aspasia's carpet on the loom. It was three-quarters finished and Christophorus remarked on its beauty.

'I want you and Saniye to continue as normal,' he told her. 'Ferit Ali is looking after us. In turn, I will make sure all the women in Stavrodromi and Pınarbaşı who continue to weave for us will be paid.'

'There are three mouths to feed in Saniye's family,' replied Aspasia. 'Soon there will be another. Fatma is pregnant.'

'Then I will give you extra for Saniye, but you must keep this between yourselves. Is that understood? If the other villagers get wind that I am favouring her over others, there will be trouble.'

After lunch, Aspasia said she would take her afternoon nap. Christophorus said he would keep his mother company for a while and then he would join her.

When the pair were alone, Marika Stavrides asked her son point blank. 'What is going to happen to the Christians, my son? The Turks have always forbidden us to have guns.'

Christophorus indicated for her to lower her voice.

'I have been informed that some are fighting whilst others will support the cause through the labour battalions.'

His mother looked puzzled.

'They will be building roads, railways, etc. Infrastructure and such like.'

Maria nodded. 'I see.'

Christophorus could see that she didn't see at all, but then neither did he.

CHAPTER 11

The Sultan Declares a Holy War

Life in Stavrodromi had always moved at a slow pace. The years slipped by with the seasons, and celebrations, and most news was gathered from the camel trains going through to cities further afield. Even life in Uşak moved at a slow pace compared to the larger cities in the empire. Many villagers had never even ventured further than Uşak itself, and those like Christophorus, Tassos, the owner of the Sun Coffee House, who had visited Alexandria and Jerusalem, and the Greek schoolteacher, Damocles, who had once been to Athens, were viewed as cosmopolitan. Now the villagers found themselves eager to learn about the outside world. When any travellers passed through the village, including the army, the locals wanted to know where they were going. Afterwards, they would clamour around a large map on the schoolroom wall and look for the places whilst Damocles, Christophorus and Tassos regaled them with stories about how many days by camel it was from the village. All the Greeks and Turks knew where Constantinople, Smyrna, Jerusalem and Mecca were, but few had any real idea about other cities in the empire.

Tassos, who by now had managed to secure his son's exemption from the army, told them about the finest coffee from the Yemen, and about spices from the east such as cardamom. Father Andronikos told them about Frankincense and Myrrh, and Jerusalem from an Orthodox perspective, whilst Imam Süleyman talked about it from an Islamic perspective, along with Mecca. Christophorus told them about Smyrna and Constantinople, and of the other big cities he had never visited himself, but knew of from his work in the carpet industry.

Thus it was that the people of Stavrodromi and Pınarbaşı managed to pull together in the face of adversity, comforting those whose menfolk had gone away, keeping an eye out for each other. The confusion began when Bekçi Baba arrived in the village with another announcement. The Sultan had declared this war to be an Islamic Holy War — on Russia and her Allies, France, Britain, Belgium, Serbia and Montenegro. The Germans and Austrians were exempt as they were now Turkey's Allies. When the head of the Islamic faith in Constantinople, presented the Sword of the Prophet to the Sultan at the Fatih Mosque, the Ottoman Christians throughout the Empire were thrown into turmoil.

The next day, several Turks went to see Imam Süleyman asking what this meant. Their immediate concern was how were they supposed to treat the Greeks in Stavrodromi?

'Do you smell the scent of the enemy in your midst? They are your brothers. Treat them with kindness.'

'But they are Christians,' one of them said, 'and I have heard Russia proclaims to look out for the Christians. We are at war with the Russians.'

'With the Russians, yes, but we are not at war with Greece and therefore not with the Greeks. Not this time. Besides, these are Greeks who have lived in Anatolia since...' Imam Süleyman thought about it. 'For longer than is written. You have known these people since you were born. Are you afraid of them?'

'Yes, that is all very well but are they not infidels?' the man continued. 'Unbelievers.'

Imam Süleyman sighed. 'You eat and drink with them. Have they not brought a fatted sheep to your celebrations, and have you not done the same for them? Keep a clean heart.'

Likewise, the Greeks of Stavrodromi sought out Father Andronikos.

'Father, what will happen to us now the Sultan has declared a Holy War against the Christians? Will the people of Pınarbaşı consider us the enemy now?'

'This jihad is not for us. It is for the enemies of the empire. You know these Turks as your friends. You have celebrated life with them and mourned the death of their loved ones. Sleep well in your beds at night, my children.'

Imam Süleyman and Father Andronikos's words were universally listened to and accepted, yet try as they would, a sense of foreboding crept into the village, as silently as the winter mists that heralded the onset of another long, cold winter.

*

Christophorus stayed a few more days in Stavrodromi. When he was not out checking the weavers' progress, he spent the rest of the time with Aspasia. Daily they walked to the church and prayed. Now more than ever, they needed God to watch over them. Aspasia lit a candle and kissed the blessed icon.

'If you can hear me, blessed Mother of Christ, please look after us and those who have left to fight.' She mumbled the soft words for longer than usual. 'I pray for Cemal also, that you will return him safe and sound to Saniye.'

She finished with another prayer. The one she said on a daily basis; that the Virgin would look kindly on her and help her to conceive again. Afterwards, she joined Christophorus outside and they took a long walk before returning home. At one point they sat on a rock and looked down at the villages below, just as she did with Saniye. A camel train arrived from the east and they could see Ancient Yusuf's two boys running around to help out. The camel herders disappeared into the coffee houses whilst their animals rested. Christophorus was thankful that Stavrodromi was on the trading route as the traders brought extra income. They would need it if the war continued.

'I wonder what news they will bring us today?' Aspasia asked. 'Let's hope it's heartening.'

Christophorus told her he would be returning to Uşak as he was sure Ferit Ali would need him.

'I need you here,' she said. 'Your presence gives us comfort.'

'There will be plenty of time for us to be together after this war is over,' he said. 'You will manage. You have my mother and Saniye.'

At the thought of Saniye, Aspasia gave a deep sigh.

'How can she still love a man like Cemal after he takes another wife and ignores her?' she asked.

'Cemal has the old ways. It can't be changed. Let's hope his being away makes the three women pull together, although I don't like the thought that Ayşe Baci is out there tending his goats. With the winter coming, it's not good for her. She looked quite frail the other day.'

'There's no-one else to do his work. Everyone is too busy looking after themselves. Thank goodness Nikos, Ilyias and Mikis either have young sons or fathers to look after their flocks.'

They returned home, stopping off to have a coffee at the Sun Coffee House first. Women did not usually frequent the coffee houses, but things had changed since the war started. Tassos now kept a few tables outside for the women. Hasan had done the same in his coffee house but the Turkish women still chose to stay away. Even if they wore the veil, it was still frowned upon for them to be seen in the company of men drinking and smoking.

Later that evening, Aspasia prepared Christophorus a special meal of roasted goat ribs and vegetables cooked in the village oven. She also wore one of her favourite embroidered robes which fastened at bodice level with plaited buttons and loops and delicate silk cord-work. It was set off by the filigree earrings and the cream shoes. The night air had chilled considerably and Christophorus made a fire in the hearth. In the soft orange glow of the flickering firelight, Aspasia looked so beautiful it took his breath away, and he even considered staying a few more days. Her glossy black hair, perfumed for the occasion with rose oil again, was braided at the back exposing the nape of her graceful neck. Christophorus put his arms around her and gently kissed it.

'My glittering one,' he whispered in her ear.

It sent shivers down her spine. She turned to face him and

stroked his cheek. Then she moved away, and slowly started to unbutton the bodice of her dress, taking everything off until she wore nothing except the cream silk slippers. At the sight of his ravishing wife with her gentle curves, small firm breasts with their erect nipples as rosy as the ripest pomegranate, dark, silken pubic hair that hid the finest fruit he had ever tasted, he pushed her gently onto the carpet and made love, passionately, wildly, and without restraint. For her part, Aspasia gave herself completely, drowning the still night air with ecstatic moans of delight. When it was over, they lay on the carpet warming their naked bodies in front of the fire. After a while, Aspasia tore herself from his embrace and went to fetch something from the other room.

'A gift for you,' she said, kneeling beside him. 'I made it myself.'

It was the red-leather embroidered document holder and like everything else she worked on, it was exquisite.

He reached out, pulled her head towards him and kissed her. His eyes looked into hers as his mouth devoured her lips.

'I shall use it with pride,' he declared, stroking the curve of her breast. 'Every time my eyes look upon it, I shall imagine they are falling on your beauty. And every time I hold it, I will be holding you, and I will think of this evening.'

Christophorus left Stavrodromi before sunrise the next morning. Sometime later, Saniye knocked on the door. Aspasia was pleased to see her and hugged her warmly.

'I cannot stay in that house a moment longer,' she said, fanning her hand in front of her face with exasperation.

Saniye did not offer an explanation as to why she had stayed away so long and Aspasia asked no questions. She was just glad to have her old friend back. After drinking a welcome bowl of warm milk, Saniye calmed down and said she was ready to weave again. The design had progressed slowly since Christophorus had been home. If they wanted to get it finished by Christmas, they had to get a move on.

She sat on the low bench next to Aspasia and examined the design again to check how the next few rows would look. When she reached up to put it back on the ledge above the balls of wool, she noticed a small silver icon there also. It had once belonged to Aspasia's *yiayia*, and her mother had given it to her as a gift when she married Christophorus. Usually it sat on a small shelf in the bedroom alongside her hand mirror, brush and comb, and vial of rose oil. Saniye gave Aspasia a momentary glance. She knew exactly why it was close by.

'I will pray for you, Sister,' she said, with a smile. 'Let us hope for good news in a sea of misery,'

CHAPTER 12

Cemal's Nightmare

Ferit Ali commented on how well Christophorus looked. The few days off had done him the world of good. Unfortunately, Christophorus could not say the same for Ferit Ali. He was aging by the day.

'Take a look at this,' he said, handing a pile of orders to Christophorus. 'The Military have asked for some of our wool. Apparently it's going to be woven into greatcoats for the solders at the Front. We are also to give over more of our looms to weaving blankets. The order is urgent and we've already started on them. Some were picked up last night.'

Christophorus asked if he knew where they were going, but was told the Military would not disclose that information.

'If it's greatcoats and blankets, it sounds like the Russian Front. Shall we do a bit of sleuth work,' he said, 'and see what we can find out at the Hotel Europa?'

Ferit Ali smiled. 'Why not? Although I fear that you will find it much changed. The Military and bureaucrats from Constantinople and Smyrna stay there now. Kyrios Lambros laments the fact that he is losing money on alcohol, and people of importance are demanding the finest which he can no longer provide due to shortages. Needless to say, Russian caviar is off the menu.'

Sotiris Lambros managed to secure them a table where they dined alone, trying to eavesdrop on nearby conversations. They finished their meal and were just about to leave when an officer walked into the room and delivered a telegram to one of his superiors on the next table. He saluted and walked away.

'What is it?' one of the man's companions asked.

'The men and supplies are to leave for Erzurum first thing tomorrow.'

Without more ado, they quickly finished their drinks and left.

'You were right,' Ferit Ali said in a low voice. 'The Russian Front.'

*

Sarıkamış, December 1914

Cemal had been on the move since he left Pınarbaşı. He had travelled first to Uşak, and then on to other some other unknown destination. Someone told him it was Samsun, another, Trabzon. As the battalion climbed higher and higher and the temperature dropped below zero, he knew they were heading for the Caucasus. For most of the journey, the soldiers slept under the stars, and at first it was cold, but bearable. Now it was impossible. Cemal had never known cold like this, not even in the harshest of Anatolian winters. How could men survive in such temperatures, he asked himself?

In the early mornings, an expansive and unbroken carpet of white clouds covered the valleys below, giving him the illusion that he was floating above the earth. He pinched himself to make sure he wasn't dreaming, or worse still, dead and in heaven. By mid morning the clouds evaporated revealing the vast mountain ranges with their soaring, craggy peaks and snow laden fertile valleys. This was the terrain of wolves, bears and vultures, and if he faltered, they would feast on him within hours. As they neared their destination, the temperatures plummeted to minus thirty degrees Celsius and the snow became deeper, almost up to two meters in some places. Even with guides, men stumbled and disappeared into crevices and vanished. There was simply no time to stop and look for them.

At the top of the mountain ranges, the landscape changed and trees became scarce. Now the men had no wood to light fires for warmth or to cook on. To make matters worse, they were in desperate need of greatcoats and blankets, and many began to succumb to frostbite and hypothermia at an alarming rate.

Cemal was becoming accustomed to the cold, but now he was sure he would die before he ever got to fire a shot in battle. He wiped away the snow and ice forming on his beard and moustache.

'What are we doing here?' he mumbled to his companion. 'Who would fight a war in a place like this and in such conditions?'

'The Cossacks are used to this weather,' the man replied, trying to muster up a painful smile. 'They eat snow for breakfast.'

'And we eat air,' Cemal added. 'Or we will do if we carry on like this much longer. There's barely enough food for two more days. Then that's it. The wolves will be circling. I heard some of the men were sent to Mesopotamia. At least it would have been warmer.'

He thought of two of the Greek shepherds from Stavrodromi, Ilyias and Nikos, at the train station in Uşak on the day he left. Apparently they were bound for Jerusalem. The idea that these two Greeks had gone to warmer climes riled him.

'Damn Christians,' he thought to himself, although he really had no idea why he would say such a thing about men he had known all his life. The propaganda about fighting a Holy War against the infidels was taking root, especially when the men were struggling beyond their endurance. 'This is madness,' Cemal declared angrily. 'Sheer madness.'

His companion tried to bolster his mood by telling him that Enver Paşa himself was fighting with them and they both agreed it must be important if the top man in the empire after the Sultan was there also. Someone shouted orders for them to get a move on. Cemal talked aimlessly to his companion, but after a while, when he didn't get a reply, he looked around and saw he was nowhere in sight.

'In the name of Allah the Almighty,' he shouted out to the stranger behind him. 'My friend, did you see him? We were together only ten minutes ago.'

The man looked at him with hollow eyes. Cemal momentarily found a burst of energy and tried to shake him.

'You must have seen him. He was right behind me.'

A voice called out again. 'Get a move on or else.'

Cemal ran around in circles like a madman. When he collapsed in the snow in tears, the officer yanked him up. 'Go on my son. Move forward or you will meet the same fate as your friend.'

The next day, the battalion reached the outskirts of the town of Sarıkamış and took up positions in the surrounding mountains, intending to fire down on the Russians who had taken the town earlier. By now most of the men who had been lucky enough to have a greatcoat at the beginning of the journey no longer had that luxury. Believing that it would slow the men down, the officers had given orders that they were to leave them behind. Cemal could not stop shaking. His face was the pallor of a ghost and his lips were turning blue. He longed for the luxury of his goatskin cape that had kept him warm during the bitterest Anatolian winters on the plateau. All around him soldiers were falling from exhaustion. It was so tempting to just curl up and go to sleep. In minutes it would all be over.

Enver Paşa gave a rallying call to the men. 'Soldiers of the Third Army, success does not come from the appearance of kit of the soldiers, but from valour and brave heart.'

Cemal had a brave heart and valour, but he was becoming delirious. The Turks began their attack and because of a lack of ammunition, rushed to the town with knives and bayonets. Cemal tried to run forward into the mêlée, but his feet were so frozen he could barely move, and he collapsed on the outskirts of town.

Despite the bravery, the Russians held on to Sarıkamış. The Turks lost 30,000 men and the Russians 28,000. Countless more died from frostbite and hypothermia. It was the first major catastrophe of the war. Long after the snow had melted and wildflowers burst forth from the fertile mountains and valleys, thousands of bodies would continue to be found.

Back in Uşak, Ferit Ali and Christophorus were working well into the night to try and fulfil the orders for the Military, but did not even scratch the surface. No sooner was one order completed than two more came in.

CHAPTER 13

A Bleak Winter

For the first time since she could remember, Aspasia spent a miserable Christmas and New Year. No-one was in the mood for celebrations. It was deemed not only inappropriate to do so when families had sent their sons to war, but the general consensus in Stavrodromi was not to antagonise their Turkish neighbours, especially with so much propaganda against the infidels. Instead, they spent more time in prayer at the Church of the Virgin, or in their homes.

Throughout December and January, the bitter cold winds swept down from the north and the Anatolian plateau was blanketed in snow. The sheep and goats were kept tethered in rudimentary huts and Ayşe Baci took to wearing Cemal's heavy goatskin cloak when she went to feed them, but the cold still seeped into her bones. With no other male in the family and Fatma pregnant, Saniye now had to help her mother-in-law with the animals, but she didn't have her tough constitution and developed a persistent cough. Aspasia worried about them all. During the summer months, the villagers conserved firewood for winter and when it ran low, it was the men who went out and found more. With the fittest away, it now fell to the old men, the young, and the women to hunt for more. The villagers were hardy, but as foodstuffs became scarce, the women began to eat less in order to keep their young ones healthy.

Christophorus had provided well for Aspasia and his mother. They had plenty of wood and sacks of dried food to draw upon. On the days that Saniye failed to show up to weave, Aspasia paid a visit to her home with a gift of food. Usually it was a bean stew, or just lately, *trachanas*, cracked wheat soaked in soured milk and dried on a table in the hot summer sun for a few days by her mother-in-law. She kept it stored it in earthenware containers in her kitchen and had more than enough to see her through winter, especially with Christophorus away. At first, it was meant to satisfy Saniye's needs, but it soon became obvious that the whole family needed her help.

She cooked a fresh pot and braved the weather to take some to Pınarbaşı. Ayşe Baci reheated the soup whilst Fatma set the low table with embroidered napkins and bowls, poured out glasses of ayran, and broke off chunks of bread from a day old loaf. To conserve wood, the village ovens were not lit every day and bread, like everything else, was a now a precious commodity. Not a crumb was wasted.

Saniye sat on the divan with a blanket wrapped around her.

'Come on, my daughter. This will do you a world of good,' Ayşe Baci told her.

Saniye's beautiful moon-face looked pale and drawn, and she welcomed the food. By all accounts, Fatma was not a good cook, and the women complained pitifully to her. Yet one look at Fatma told Aspasia that she also had problems. Her pregnancy showed, but the girl had lost weight. In fact, underneath her voluminous pantaloons and embroidered waistcoat, she was skin and bones.

Except for the continuous jangle of Fatma's many bracelets and the occasional braying of a donkey, the four women ate their meal in silence. Afterwards, Ayşe Baci made them tea, which they drank with sesame-covered, sweet biscuits prepared by Marika Stavrides.

Saniye apologised for not pulling her weight with the weaving.

'Don't worry,' Aspasia replied. 'I can manage alone. For now, you must concentrate on getting better. My house is warm, and it's not good for you to venture out in this weather.'

She turned her attention to Fatma. 'What ails you so, dear girl?'

Fatma's face reddened and she reached for her veil to hide her embarrassment. Her engraved and coral studded, silver rings glinted against her dark skin and black eyes.

'Do you have morning sickness or pains,' Aspasia asked.

Fatma shook her head. 'No Kyria.'

'Fatma, please call me Aspasia. I am a friend.'

'I'm sorry.'

'There's nothing to apologise for. I'm trying to help. If you are ill, maybe we can all help. Your mother-in-law helped me once you know, before you came here. I will always be indebted to her for her kindness.' She glanced at Ayşe Baci. 'What do you say? Is there anything we can do for her?'

The old woman shrugged her shoulders. Clearly no-one wanted to say what was wrong.

Aspasia left shortly after. It was late afternoon, the sky was the palest dove grey and the snow was falling again. Soft, wet snowflakes floated down from the heavens, collecting on her eyelashes and shawl which she pulled over her face for protection. The streets were cleared of snow daily, yet they were soon covered with a light dusting of fresh snow that deepened throughout the night. The glistening snow collected on rooftops dotted here and there with stork's nests, and settled in drifts against the stone walls. Above all, it was the stillness that Aspasia noticed; a peace that cloaked the villages and gave the illusion that they were safe in an unsafe world. She followed a set of fresh footprints until they disappeared at the entrance to the mosque, and continued past the snow-laden orange trees until she reached the meydan. There were no caravan trains that day and it was deserted. The only sign of life were the flickering candles through the windows of the coffee houses where the old men gathered playing backgammon, whilst waiting for news from the outside world.

Before going home, Aspasia called at her mother-in law's house. Marika Stavrides had been busy with her weaving and was glad of the company.

'Did they enjoy it?' she asked, referring to the *trachanas*.

'They did, and I think it will do them good. They thanked you for the biscuits.'

Aspasia took off her shawl and hung it near the fire to dry. 'They are all struggling. I am sure Saniye will get better when the spring thaw arrives, but it is the young girl that worries me. She is skin and bones.'

'I haven't seen her for a while,' Marika said, 'but from what Ayşe Baci tells me, the girl doesn't want this child.'

Aspasia thought of both her own longing for a child, and Saniye's.

'Isn't it strange how fate works?' Aspasia replied, warming her hands by the fire. 'Saniye is desperate for a child and this one doesn't want it. I wonder why not.'

'Perhaps someone has put a curse on her.'

Aspasia couldn't believe what she was hearing. 'Surely you don't believe that do you? It's preposterous. Saniye would never...'

'Not Saniye, Ayşe Baci. She's a dark horse that one and she *is* known to be a good healer, but what do we know about her other skills?'

Aspasia thought of the potion Ayşe Baci made that had eased her through the miscarriage, yet she couldn't conceive of her of doing anything against her own family.

'No, I'm sorry. I cannot believe that. It must be an illness or the girl is not eating. The weather doesn't help, although it's warm enough in the house.'

'Ayşe Baci despises the girl and she adores Saniye. The poor child knows that. With Cemal gone, who knows what she will do. I know Saniye is your friend, but it's better to stay out of it. Now enough of this talk, tell me, what do you think of my carpet? I have a small border to do, and then it's finished.'

Aspasia congratulated her. 'It's beautiful.'

She looked at it closely, examining the pile and then the back, which they had always been told should be just as beautiful as the pile.

'You are an exceptional weaver,' she replied. 'It will fetch a good price.'

Marika Stavrides smiled. 'I might be good, my daughter, but I am not as skilled as you. This latest one you have been working on beats all those I saw at the factory.'

Aspasia blushed. 'You are too kind. It would have been finished now if Saniye hadn't taken ill. Never-the-less, it will be finished soon, and I can't wait to start another. Christophorus already has the designer drawing up a similar one. Let's hope they find buyers for them and the work continues.'

CHAPTER 14

Mehmet's Letter to Saniye (1)

March 3, 1915

My beloved sister,

I am writing to you from a hospital bed in Çanakkale. I don't remember how I came to be here, but thanks be to Allah the Almighty, I am alive and well and on the road to recovery. On February 25th, the batteries at Kumkale and Seddülbahir were bombarded. That is where I sustained my injury.

My battalion was posted to this area because we believed the infidels were about to invade and try to conquer our beloved Istanbul. They have already taken over the ports on Lemnos and Imbros. You can imagine the distress this has caused us, but we have spent weeks fortifying the defences along this stretch of coastline and are ready for them. Mines have been laid in the Narrows and the forts are well fortified. I was given the task of stretching barbed wire across the beaches and under the water. You will recall that I have *a fear of water since falling in the Bosphorus as a child, but what could I do? Such times called for me to put my childish fears behind me and act like a man.*

The Kaiser, may Allah praise his goodness, has not only supplied us with skilled soldiers, but we also have the best weapons. I would love to see the Infidels' faces when they discover we have cleverly camouflaged heavy guns which we call "Krupp Monsters", south of Conk Bayiri. Whatever is going through their minds, let them be assured that we will defend our land to the last man.

March 10

The weather has been pitiful but that will not last. Soon it will be spring, and the hills will be filled with the beauty of wildflowers, and I fear, the blood of brave men. Today we heard that the Greeks tried to join the war, but the Russians have vetoed the idea. I suspect they also have eyes on that great city captured by our beloved Mehmet the Conqueror. If the Greeks join the war, it will be a disaster.

And now, my dearest sister, I must take my rest. I am in good spirits and expect to be back with my battalion in the next day or two. Pray for me as I pray for you,

Your beloved brother,

Mehmet

CHAPTER 15

Aspasia receives a French Clock

It was three months to the day when Saniye received Mehmet's letter. Somehow, it made its way into Christophorus's hands at The Anatolian Carpet Manufacturers Ltd. As he could not read Turkish, it was Ferit Ali who told him it was intended for "Saniye, wife of Cemal, goatherd of Pınarbaşı". He gave it to Aspasia to give to her, and she asked the scribe to read it on his next visit to the village. Although Mehmet never told her what his injuries were, Saniye took heart from the fact that if he was returning to his battalion, then he was alright. But she did bear the guilt of not being able to send him more money. If she had, he wouldn't have gone to war in the first place.

Mehmet's prophecy came true. The Allies landed their expeditionary forces on the Gallipoli Peninsula on April 25. 1915. It was on such a scale that it could not be kept from the people. With the defeat of Basra, Sarıkamış, and the Suez at the beginning of February, the survival of the empire now rested on what was taking place on the Gallipoli Peninsula. Constantinople and the empire were on tenterhooks. Defeat was not an option.

Throughout the winter of 1915, several more caravan trains passed through the villages. Each time they stopped and took refreshments in the coffee houses. Some of the traders still came from the east but as the weeks passed, more caravans headed eastwards towards Damascus, Jerusalem and Mesopotamia laden with vital necessities for the war effort. Because of the position of Stavrodromi and Pınarbaşı on the trading route, Tassos and Hasan put in a special request to the officials in Uşak to be able to buy coffee, sugar and tobacco. They argued it was their duty to supply such things in order to keep up the morale, especially those fighting in the service of the empire. Their pleas worked, and they were granted a special dispensation on the grounds that it was only to be served to the Military and none went to the villagers. They were taken to a supply warehouse and made to sign for the goods at hugely inflated prices. Their first instinct was to barter, but their survival instinct told them to pay quickly and leave before the officials changed their minds.

With the oxcart laden with goods, Tassos and Hasan returned home in high spirits but this did not last long. When they entered the valley and heard the sound of drums, they looked at each other. Bekçi Baba had paid another visit calling for more men. This time six more men prepared to leave for Uşak. The women were wailing, and no amount of cajoling by officials about duty in the name of Allah, the Sultan or the Empire would stop them.

Once again, Markos, Vassilis the Greek grocer's son, was called up, as was Thanassos. Markos showed the official his exemption paper stating that he had only recently paid for this. Thanassos did the same, but the official merely shrugged his shoulders and said there was nothing he could do about. The names were on the list and that was that.

When Tassos arrived, he came to his son's defence, but it was to no avail. He was told that he would have to reapply again.

'I am sorry,' the official said. 'Take it up with the authorities in Uşak.'

'If I have to pay another fee for my son, it will finish me,' Vassilis said to Tassos. 'I have nothing to sell these days, and no more income.'

Tassos had his own problems. He had just outlaid a small fortune on goods, and it would take a while to recover that before he made a small profit again. The Turkish grocer overheard Vassilis and smiled to himself. Now the Greek's son would be forced to join up just as his own son had done.

The next day, Tassos returned to Uşak with Thanassos to pay the last of his savings on another exemption fee. This time it had increased. They called by The Anatolian Carpet Manufacturers Ltd. to visit Christophorus and see if he had any news on the war that everyone expected to be over by now. Sadly, he could tell them little. His carpet contacts had told him that the British, who already had obtained navigation rights to sail the Euphrates and Tigris from the Porte years ago, had managed to secure the region south of Basra and were heading towards Baghdad, but he still did not know the extent of the losses at Sarıkamış. He did promise to see what he could do about getting Thanassos a job in Uşak — something of importance which meant his skills would be invaluable at home and exempt him from military service.

'I am not skilled at anything, except helping my father in the coffee house,' Thanassos replied, with a hollow laugh.

'Leave it with me,' Christophorus replied. 'I'll think of something.' He reached for his wallet, counted out the equivalent of the exemption fee, and handed it to Tassos.

'I can't take this,' Tassos replied. 'It wouldn't be right.'

'Take it, I insist. It's a gift. When your son gets a job, he can pay me back. For now use it to buy coffee or goods from the traders. Who knows what tomorrow will bring?'

*

Aspasia was sitting by the Fountain of the Sun and Moon, soaking up the afternoon sun and chatting to other women when Christophorus unexpectedly arrived home. With him were two men leading several mules laden with sacks of wool. Ancient Yusuf sent his two boys to help them up the steep and narrow cobble-stoned street to the house, and after depositing the sacks inside the gate, returned to the meydan to feed the animals.

'What's all this?' Aspasia asked. 'We've just had a new batch of wool and the carpets we're working on won't be ready for some time.'

'I'll explain soon enough,' Christophorus replied. 'For now, I must see that these good men get a bite to eat before returning to Uşak.'

Leaving Aspasia to ponder what the wool was for, the men headed back to the meydan and the Sun Coffee House. Tassos shook his hand warmly.

'What brings you back?' he asked. 'We weren't expecting you until the weekend.'

'There are a few things I had to attend to. Firstly, I have

secured Thanassos a position with the Uşak Municipal Lighting Co. He starts straight away. I will be returning tomorrow. He can come with me.'

Tassos looked stunned. 'But I thought those jobs were all taken. Besides, Thanassos would need training. Are you sure?'

'It's all arranged. There are Greeks working there who have promised to take him under their wing. To all intents and purposes, he is well qualified. That's all he needs to remember. Now, if you will excuse me, I must get back home. Please see to it that these men get a good breakfast before they return to Uşak.'

Aspasia was in the process of opening the sacks when Christophorus walked in. Each one contained the colours she worked her designs in.

'What's going on?' she asked, holding up a skein of dark red wool in one hand and a blue one in the other. 'I already have enough wool for this carpet. Why have you brought more, and why in the middle of the week?'

Christophorus took the wool from her and sat her down.

'I have something important to tell you but it mustn't go any further than this room. Do you understand? I don't even want my mother to know.'

'Christophorus, you're frightening me.'

'These sacks were left in my office yesterday. I was out all day and found them when I returned in the evening. There was an envelope on top of one of them addressed to me. It was from Sara.'

Aspasia looked confused. 'Is she alright?'

'No. I fear not. She left suddenly.'

'And she didn't say anything?'

Christophorus deliberated over his words.

'Most of the Armenians have left Uşak. They were given twenty-four hours to put their affairs in order and go.'

'Go where?'

'I'm not sure, but I believe it's somewhere in the East. Ferit Ali told me the government wants them away from the war zones. They have it on good authority that they are aiding the Russians. Many have deserted or gone over to the other side, and they believe there are sleeper cells ready to revolt. Their travel documents have been suspended, and anyone suspecting of insurrection is to be executed.'

'Are you sure?'

'These are not rumours, my love. This time it's serious. Ferit Ali learnt of this when he was in Constantinople. His relative is an official with the Ministry of the Interior. On the evening of the Allied landings on the Gallipoli Peninsula, the authorities rounded up over a hundred Armenian notables in Constantinople.'

Aspasia could scarcely believe what she was hearing. 'Are you saying all the Armenians have left? What about the weavers? Half of them are Armenian.'

Christophorus reached for a bottle of raki, poured out a full glass and drank it in one go.

'It has decimated the industry,' he replied, wiping his mouth with the back of his hand. 'I don't know how we will survive, especially with half of the work being produced for the Military.'

The last few months Aspasia had fretted that she had still been unable to conceive, but this latest news shocked her to the core. The war was encroaching on their life more and more.

'From what I hear, the battles on the Gallipoli Peninsula are taking an enormous toll on lives and no one knows what will happen. Losses on the Russian Front and in Mesopotamia have made the Porte nervous.'

'What does Sara have to do with what's going on in the East? None of her relatives live there.'

Christophorus sighed. 'I know, but the authorities want them away from the war zones.' He saw the look in her eyes and wondered if it had been a wise decision to tell her. 'She'll be alright, my darling.'

'What about us, Christophorus? Where does that leave us?' Aspasia asked, nervously poking a long strand of hair back behind her ear.

'Greece has not joined the war, so we have nothing to fear.' He took her hand and kissed it. 'My precious one, you are safe here. Don't worry.'

Aspasia turned her attention to the wool. 'And all this?'

'The note said it was for your carpets. Sara made sure you would have enough for several more should wool become scarce.'

There was one more unopened sack by the door and Christophorus dragged it into the room.

'And in here,' he said, untying the string, 'are your new designs. She had been working on them for the last few months, and wanted to be sure you got them.'

He reached into the middle of the sack and pulled out a long roll wrapped in newspaper. Inside were designs based on old Uşak carpets that she had copied from engravings and photographs of originals, except that Sara's were much better: a slight tweak here and there to a bird motif, a small diamond in a lozenge shape, an extra border, etc. They were exquisite.

'There's one more thing.'

He reached down further into the sack and brought out a clock. Aspasia brought her hand to her mouth. 'In the name of the Virgin, where did you get that?

'It's a gift. When I found out what was taking place, I went straight away to Sara's home. The family had already left, but a neighbour recognised me and pulled me inside. Sara had left a package with her, and she was going to bring it to the factory when things died down. It's a token of thanks — something to remember her by.'

It was a French mantle clock about 35cm in height, and it clearly looked out of place in their simple home.

'It's stunning, but it belongs in a palace,' Aspasia replied, taking it from him and examining the fine details. 'Look, it even has the name of the clockmaker on the back –"Pons" of Paris. Do you know how old it is?'

'Ferit Ali has one in his home, and I've also seen a similar one at the Hotel Europa. I would say it's almost a hundred years old.'

Aspasia wiped it gently with a cloth and stood it on its base.

'It must be worth a small fortune. Surely she could have sold it and used the money.'

'The neighbour told me the family gave an inventory of all the goods left behind to an official but this wasn't on it.'

'Where are we going to put it?' Aspasia asked, still in shock at receiving such a gift

They scanned the room for the appropriate place, but nothing seemed worthy of something so fine, so for the time being they sat it on an embroidered cloth on the floor. Christophorus promised to buy a nice piece of furniture for it as soon as he returned to Uşak.

Sara's sudden departure along with the other Armenian weavers in the factory cast a shadow of melancholia over their evening, but Aspasia tried hard to enjoy the short time with Christophorus, who she noticed was drinking more than usual. In an effort to cheer him up, she slipped into a beautiful robe and wore her cream slippers which always put him in a good mood.

'Let's eat outside,' she said. 'The weather is perfect. The air is warm and filled with the scent of flowers. It will do you good.'

That night they dined on stuffed aubergines followed by cinnamon and orange infused halva. Afterwards, Christophorus brought out their bedroll and they lay in each other's arms under the loquat tree. This year the succulent orange-fleshed fruit had been profuse, and Aspasia had made conserves and spoon-fruits, and exchanged some for Saniye's mulberry jam. Now it was filled with tiny buds which would develop into small clusters that would burst open into creamy-white flowers with the first autumn chill.

The world around them was in turmoil but just for that one moment in time, they were able to put it all behind them and savour each other's company. With the full moon looking down on them from above, they took pleasure in each other's body until finally, enveloped in a heady combination of passion and perfumed night air, they fell into a deep and peaceful sleep.

CHAPTER 16

Fatma

A few weeks later, Sara's clock took pride of place on a small, walnut cabinet with two shelves and an engraved glass door that Christophorus had bought at a bargain price from the sale of Armenian furniture left behind. He never knew who it belonged to and didn't ask. Aspasia was thrilled with it as she could now display her set of fine coffee cups, resplendent with delicate gold and enamel eggcup-shaped stands. The clock became cause for much delight by the women of Stavrodromi and Pınarbaşı who would call round for tea just to sit and look at it. The visits were always well-timed to allow for ample chatter and drink tea as they listened to its mesmerizing ticking sound. But the real joy came when it chimed beautifully on the hour. At that point they would giggle and clap like schoolgirls and then take their leave. Such were the simple joys that could still be found when their menfolk were away at war.

*

During the first weeks of summer, Fatma went into labour. It was a painful breach birth and neither she nor the child was strong enough to cope. The child was stillborn and Fatma died the following day of complications. With no money to hire a professional washer, Saniye and Ayşe Baci took her body into the garden and laid her out under the mulberry tree. After washing her three times, they wrapped her in a simple white cloth and secured it with a rope. The new-born was wrapped in a tiny bundle and laid beside her. Ayşe Baci, tinged with remorse at the way she had treated her second daughter-in-law, fetched Imam Süleyman to say a few prayers in order that Fatma would be rewarded in Paradise on the Day of Judgement. Afterwards she paid four old men from the village to carry the body to the Islamic cemetery behind Pınarbaşı and bury it. A simple stone marked the spot where she lay.

Fatma had died in the early hours of the morning and by afternoon prayers, she was in the earth. There was no wake and no-one shed any tears, especially not Saniye and Ayşe Baci. Neither would they observe the forty days of mourning. Only on the fortieth day, did they go to the mosque to say a prayer, more in the hope that Allah would forgive their sins than for Fatma. In a village where the rituals of life and death played such an important part of life, it was as if Fatma had never existed.

*

By the time the men from The Anatolian Carpet Maufacturers Ltd. came to collect the next batch of carpets, Aspasia and Saniye were back in the swing of things again. For Saniye,

Fatma had been a constant reminder of her failure as a woman to provide Cemal with a child, and even though the girl had died under terrible circumstances, she was happy once more. She vowed to herself that if Cemal returned home, she would be the woman he had once loved and perhaps this time, Allah the Almighty would look more favourably on her and she would give him a child.

But for Ayşe Baci, tending her son's goats soon took its toll. Throughout the winter she could find no relief from the cold and her body was constantly racked with pain. The added hardship she endured through food shortages meant that her body was malnourished and even Cemal's heavy goat-hair cloak no longer afforded warmth. Now that summer was here, she suffered in other ways. The relentless heat brought dust and flies. When she came home in the evening, she was too exhausted to weave. Fatma had made several attempts to weave, but her work was uneven and sloppy and Ayşe Baci was so embarrassed she destroyed it. In the end the loom stood idle.

*

By now, most of the new recruits were being sent to the Gallipoli Peninsula where fighting was at its heaviest. For many, they had never ventured further than their local villages or the nearest big town and had no idea what to expect. The closer they got, the more apprehensive they became. Desertion was not an option. The gendarmes were everywhere and deserters were summarily executed which caused great shame and hardship to the family. One such person was a man from the next village who was found hiding in the caravanserai by Ancient

119

Yusuf. The gendarmes arrived soon after and he was executed in the meydan as an example to others. It was the first public execution the villagers had witnessed and for weeks afterwards, no one could bring themselves to mention it.

CHAPTER 17

Mehmet's Letter to Saniye (2)

Conk Bayiri, August 15, 1915

My dearest sister,

It is hard for me to describe what we have been through over the last few months, suffice to say that thanks be to Allah the Almighty, I am still alive. Our soldiers are now under the command of Colonel Mustafa Kemal, commander of the 19th Division, and it is due to him that we are finally defeating the infidels. He orders us to die but does nothing which he would not do himself. Indeed, such a man of profound courage, I have never met before. Every day for the past few weeks, I watched him standing on the ridge, looking though his binoculars from his observation post or consulting his map and compass. He shows no fear and inspires such spirit in us. When he instructs us, we fix our bayonets and leap into the darkness like lions, swarming down the hillside and calling out 'Allah! Allah!'

The attacks have been relentless and with such ferocity that our nerves are constantly on edge. This is a wicked war, and I have seen my fellow soldiers cut into pieces beside me. When I close my eyes for a few brief hours, I hear the tic-tac of machine guns, the rattle of rifles, and the roar of big guns. Added to all this confusion are the cries of the wounded. So many men who cry for their mothers, it is pitiful. And for us still alive, there is the added misery of dysentery, malaria, flies and lice.

The enemy fares no better. Occasionally one of them throws us a tin of something called "Bully beef" in exchange for cigarettes, but it does not compare with the occasional eggs and fresh yoghurt that the villagers supply us. Once or twice I have thrown them a few walnuts. We are all grateful for what we can get because none of us know what tomorrow will bring. This is what our life has become.

My dearest, sister, you are constantly in my thoughts and I pray for the day when I will see your lovely face once more. Without the fighting, this place is quite beautiful. Steep hills cover the scrubby undergrowth and sweep down to the deep blue water. In spring the wildflowers blossomed in profusion, but this year, the beauty of the Gallipoli Rose, anemones and pink Catchfly were soon stained in the blood of the enemy and our own men — courageous men who will be remembered long after the peninsula has ceased to be a place of killing fields.

Pray for me as I pray for you,
Your beloved brother,
Mehmet.

Mehmet's letter was delivered to Saniye at the onset of winter, in 1915. With it was another letter of a more official nature. The second simply stated that Mehmet, son of Ibrahim the shoemaker, Street of the Shoemakers, Galata, died serving the Sultan and the Empire on 20th April 1915. His body was laid to rest on the heights of Sari Bayir Ridge.

CHAPTER 18

A Son of Pınarbaşı Returns Home.

1916 was a bleak year. The infidels had finally left the Gallipoli Peninsula and the Turks were victorious. With this victory, the name on everyone's lips was that of Mustafa Kemal Bey. He had a shining star over him and was destined for glory. No-one knew where that glory would end, but such was his fame and presence that all who knew him came under his spell. Some said it was his eyes, others his clear thinking. Whatever it was, he inspired greatness and determination in those who met him. Elsewhere, the war was not going well and the villagers of Stavrodromi and Pınarbaşı struggled to survive. Then something unexpected happened: Cemal returned.

Word of his imminent arrival from Uşak soon reached the villages, and by the time the oxcart trundled into the meydan, all the villagers were there to greet him. Being the first man to return from war, Cemal's arrival was met with great fanfare. The verandas of the Sun Coffee house and the Coffee House of the moon were decked out in Turkish Flags and both Tassos and Hasan declared drinks were on the house, even though they were barely making ends meet. The children ran around waving Turkish flags, whilst the Turkish women made high-pitched trilling sounds to the drums and flutes played by the old men. If Cemal could make it back, then that was cause for optimism.

Someone rode out by donkey onto the plateau to give Ayşe Baci the good news whilst Aspasia helped Saniye dress in her finest clothes — a pair of brightly coloured, voluminous pantaloons tied at the waist with a wide belt and ornate silver belt buckle, and an embroidered waistcoat. On her head, she exchanged her usual red kerchief for a large yellow one edged with ribbon embroidery and silver coins that sat low on her forehead emphasizing her dark arched brows. Finally she put on a pair of pendulous silver earrings. In less than two hours, she had had transformed herself to the moon-faced beauty that she had been before Fatma arrived.

When the cart trundled into view, the young children ran to escort it until it stopped next to the Fountain of the Sun and Moon. The villagers crowded around, pushing and shoving to welcome their hero back, but as two men helped Cemal get down from the cart, the joy quickly turned to despair. A hush descended and the villagers stared in horror. Cemal could barely walk.

Ayşe Baci pushed her way through the throng towards her son and instinctively knelt down to kiss his feet. Suddenly she reeled back in fright, shrieking and beating her chest like a madwoman. Saniye ran up behind her and after seeing the state her husband, collapsed on the ground in a faint.

The Cemal who had left Pınarbaşı — a fit and healthy man in the prime of his life — was not the same man who had returned. The appalling conditions of the Sarıkamış Campaign had extracted a terrible toll on him. He had lost both his feet to frostbite as well as several fingers on his left hand. His face was blotched in varying shades of red to bluish purple and was peeling badly, and his eyesight had deteriorated from snow blindness. In that moment, the villagers only saw the physical scars; in reality, his mental scars were far worse.

*

Even though Cemal was very much alive, the villagers wept for him. As for Cemal himself, he refused to talk about the war. *What's the point of trying to tell them what I endured? They can't possibly understand,* he said to himself as he sat under the mulberry tree, drinking endless cups of sugarless tea prepared by his doting mother and the woman who called herself his 'true wife'. Their chatter bored him and his thoughts turned inwards. *Was it worth it, shedding all that blood in the name of the Sultan? Damn those men who sent us to our deaths. May they never see Paradise.*

Ayşe Baci returned to the plateau, but the thought that she would spend the rest of her days tending the animals instead of weaving was more than she could bear. She sought solace in prayer or concocting potions to heal her sick son. She had always been a good healer, especially with "women's issues", but nothing would bring back her son's feet and fingers. Her small kitchen was now spilling over with bunches of dried herbs and blossoms, jars of seeds, and potions of some sort or other fermenting on the hearth and window sill. Every day before she left for the plateau, she issued detailed orders to

125

Saniye on what to do with her concoctions and ointments. *Sari kantaron*, similar to St. John's-Wort, which had been left to sit in olive oil for fifteen days until it turned a fire-red, was to be rubbed on the skin to heal scarring; eggplant cooked in ashes and mixed with powdered henna was used for his eczema and blotched skin, and she was to bathe him in barley water twice a day. As if that wasn't enough, whenever Ayşe came across a hedgehog, she brought it home and ground the meat which she made into cigar-shaped pastries for his eczema. The only thing she couldn't cure was his depression, but it was not for want of trying. This time *Sari kantaron* was used as a tisane. At the back of her mind, Ayşe Baci really believed Cemal was cursed because of her. She had taken great care that not even Saniye knew of the potions she gave to Fatma that aided the girl's demise. In fact she had thrown away the evidence before the girl died because Saniye was asking too many questions. But *He* must have seen her. Allah the all-seeing, the all knowing one; *He* knew, and now she was paying for her actions. Why else should they have such ill luck?

Night and day, the women tended to Cemal's needs. Saniye confided in Aspasia that she still loved him, even though he was a shell of a man.

'Has he asked about Fatma?' Aspasia asked.

Saniye shook her head. 'Not once.'

'Wouldn't it be better to tell him what happened?'

'I have discussed it with my mother-in-law. She forbids any mention of her. We will wait to see if he brings it up. For the moment, I pray for him to get better and love me as he used to. Any talk of Fatma may ignite old wounds.'

Aspasia sensed that Saniye still held on to the hope that she would one day have a child. If that was so, who was she to cast a shadow over such desires when she was in the same position herself.

CHAPTER 19

Christophorus leaves Uşak

The French clock chimed twelve o'clock. The women clapped and then departed back to their homes leaving Aspasia to wash up the tea cups and make herself lunch. Today, it would be *horta* gathered the day before from the area around the Church of the Virgin. After boiling it for a few minutes, she emptied it out onto a platter, placed a thick slice of goat's cheese on top of it with a few black olives and scattered a little dried oregano over the top. Finally she dribbled olive oil over it followed by a squeeze of lemon. Times might be difficult but she was thankful to still eat a cheap and nourishing meal.

She was half way through when there was a knock on the door. Wondering who would call at such a time, she wiped her mouth with her napkin and answered it. It was Tassos and the school teacher, Damocles.

'Can we come in for a moment, Kyria Stavrides,' Tassos said. 'We have something important to tell you.'

Aspasia indicated for them to sit down and poured them a glass of apricot juice.

'There's no easy way to say this,' Tassos said. 'We've just received word that Greece has declared war on Germany and her Allies. That means Bulgaria and the Ottoman Empire.'

The blood drained from Aspasia's face. The first thing that came to her mind was that the Porte would view the Greeks in the same light as the Armenians — trouble makers — and she had a vision of them all being sent east, as far away from Greece as possible.

'What does this mean?' she asked, her eyes darting from one to another.

'We will be targeted, that's for sure, just in case any of us have allegiances to Greece,' Damocles replied.

'Why should we? We have been loyal subjects.'

He gave a long sigh. 'I am afraid that there are groups in the big cities — Constantinople and Smyrna, for instance, who have covertly been working to undermine the Ottoman Empire and they would like nothing better than to join the Greek cause. Take their Prime Minister for instance, Eleftherios Venizelos; now there's a man who is determined to see that this happens and he has influential friends amongst the European powers.'

Aspasia looked perplexed. 'None of this makes sense. I have never understood how we ended up in this mess in the first place. Look at us, we mind our own business and then all this happens. Christophorus always said you can't trust politicians.'

At the thought of Christophorus, she crossed herself. 'Do you think he will be alright?'

Tassos and Damocles looked at each other. Who was the one who was going to deliver the bad news?

'We were about to come to that. Christophorus has been called up. He has forty-eight hours to get his things in order, and the authorities won't let him leave Uşak in case he doesn't return. Thanassos is in the same boat. He has also been called up. It's the third time now, and I haven't the money to save him. Even if I had, I doubt they would let him off the hook this time. I'm leaving for Uşak as soon as possible to see what I can do. Christophorus has sent word for you to go with me. He needs to see you.'

Aspasia felt faint and her legs started to buckle. Damocles caught her in time.

'You must be strong, Kyria Stavrides.'

'You are right,' she replied fanning herself with the napkin. 'Please excuse me.'

After making sure she would be alright, the two men left the house, leaving Aspasia to prepare for her departure. They decided it was better not to tell Christophorus's mother any of this yet. There was no use in worrying her unnecessarily. Aspasia feared she might want to accompany them to Uşak herself, and that would only add to Christophorus's dilemma.

A few hours later, Tassos helped Aspasia onto the oxcart, and the pair departed for Uşak.

*

It had been a while since Aspasia had been to Uşak. The town she remembered had always been one of commerce: a lively, thriving place where people of all nationalities gathered to do business or socialize in the coffee houses from early morning until late at night. Now the dark clouds of war descended over it. Soldiers carrying rifles and backpacks had replaced the merchants and business men, and instead of commercial goods, the camel and mule trains transported supplies of ammunition. Turkish flags hung from buildings and trees, and heavy field guns trundled through the streets churning up the roads into deep tracts of mud that made it difficult to walk.

When they passed the railway station, a Military band was serenading a large group of new recruits waiting to be deployed to wherever the next offensive was planned. All bore a look of fear or emptiness. What the fate of these men would be, only God knew. Aspasia wanted Tassos to stop whilst she looked to see if she recognised any the men, but, seeing that the area was heavily guarded by gendarmes, Tassos thought it unwise to hang around.

Christophorus was in his office sorting out a mound of papers when they entered. Aspasia ran to him and he held her tightly. He looked pale and tired.

'In the name of the Virgin,' she cried, 'Please tell me you don't have to go. There must be some mistake. I thought Ferit Ali had it all sorted.'

At the sight of his distraught wife, Christophorus struggled to maintain an air of composure.

'I tried, my precious one,' he replied, stroking her face. 'God knows, I tried. As soon as I was notified I went to the recruiting officer with my exemption papers again, but this time it wasn't enough. That damn Abdullah, may God Almighty strike him down, just laughed in my face. I handed him another envelope and told him that this time I'd doubled the amount. He emptied the money on to the desk and I watched as his fat fingers, laden with gold and gem-studded rings, counted it out in front of me. Then he laughed in my face and pocketed it.

'"Do you think you can bribe me like this?" he said. "You

Greeks are all the same — scum!" When I brought up the fact that I had worked tirelessly to fulfil the Military's orders, he was unmoved and said Ferit Ali will have to find someone else.'

Aspasia's eyed filled with tears. 'How long have you got?' she asked, her voice shaking with fear.

'A few hours. There's a train leaving this evening and I must be on it.'

'Do you know where they're sending you?'

'Not yet.'

'I shall not sleep at night wondering where you are and if you're safe.'

'Ferit Ali knows someone at the railway station. He will inform him where we are heading and get word to you. At least that should help to put your mind at rest.'

'And Thanassos?' asked Tassos, who until this point, had been standing quietly by the door. 'Where can I find him? I must see him before he leaves.'

'I'm sorry, Tasso. It's too late. He left this morning. All I know is there were other Greeks with him and the train was heading to Ayfon.'

Tassos walked over to the window and stared outside, his face impassive. He was a man used to hiding his emotions, but this news struck him like a dagger to the heart. He tried to speak, but the words would not come.

'We tried, my friend,' Christophorus said, putting a comforting hand on his shoulder 'I doubled his fee also.'

Tassos wondered if one of the new recruits at the station might have been his son, and hated himself for not wanting to stop as Aspasia had suggested.

'You have done everything in your power to help him,' he

replied, 'and for that I am indebted to you, but this time, the fates are against us.'

There was little more Tassos could do or say except pray for his son's safe return. Under the pretence of needing fresh air, he excused himself to wait outside leaving Aspasia and Christophorus to say their goodbyes in private.

'I have something to give you,' Christophorus said to Aspasia when they were alone.

He took a pair of keys out of the top drawer of his desk and asked her to follow him to Ferit Ali's office. Ferit Ali was at the Europa trying to find a replacement for Christophorus and would probably not be back until later. One of the keys opened his office door and the other was for the hidden safe in the back room.

'Should we be here?' Aspasia asked anxiously. 'What if he comes back? He'll think we're snooping around?'

'It's fine. He gave me the keys on purpose, should anything happen. That time has come.'

When they entered the back room, he pushed the chest of drawers away from the wall and unlocked the safe. The box still contained a large amount of cash.

Aspasia stared in disbelief as he grabbed several handfuls and quickly stuffed them into the red leather document holder she had made him. Then, he quickly locked the safe and pushed the drawers back into place.

'This is for you. Keep it somewhere safe. Should anything happen to me, there's enough to see you right for a few years.'

Aspasia could scarcely comprehend what was happening. 'But... does Ferit Ali know about this?' she said, her voice choking with emotion.

'It was his idea. I was to use this money as I saw fit. I've already used quite a bit on exemption fees. He knows that.'

'Won't you need it where you're going to?'

'Don't worry. I already have some. I sewed it into the lining of my jacket.'

He opened the front of his jacket wide to show her. 'I thought I did a good job,' he said with a smile. 'You'd never notice would you?'

'This is not a joking matter,' Aspasia said, curtly.

'No it certainly isn't,' Christophorus replied. 'I wish it was. Now let's get back to Tassos.'

Tassos was pacing the empty yard like a caged animal. He was a big, solid brute of a man who had been a wrestler in his youth, but now he looked like a vulnerable overgrown child and it was evident from his red eyes that he'd shed a tear or two.

'We'd best get back to Stavrodromi before sunset,' he said to Christophorus. 'You can rest assured I will keep a close eye on Aspasia and your mother.'

'Thank you. I know they will be safe in your care.'

It was useless to delay the goodbyes any longer. None of this was doing any of them any good and there were things Christophorus needed to attend to before his departure.

'Take good care, my darling,' Aspasia said, tears streaking her face. 'And remember, I will love you till the day I die. Not even death will part us.'

Christophorus cupped her face and gave her a long lingering kiss. Funny, he thought to himself, how the kiss of parting is the sweetest kiss of all. In that moment, he breathed in everything about her: the rose-oil in her hair, the saltiness of her saliva, the fragrance of her skin — even the sweet taste and delicate smell of her sex. It was all there in that one kiss. Those were the memories that would keep him going.

He tore himself from her grasp and shook Tassos's hand firmly. Then he turned on his heels and went inside.

Aspasia started to run after him but Tassos stopped her.

'Be strong. If not for yourself, for him.'

Tassos tethered Christophorus's horse to the cart with instructions that Ancient Yusuf was to take care of it until he returned. Life had dealt them a bitter blow and they just had to make the best of it.

CHAPTER 20

Aspasia takes a Lesson in Politics

As if to echo her mood, the sky darkened to a dull, slate grey, and the first of the winter snows started to fall. Aspasia wrapped a few biscuits in a cloth, rugged herself up and headed to the schoolhouse. She timed it just right. The children had all gone home and Damocles was alone. The schoolhouse consisted of one large room with a few rudimentary wooden desks for the children and a larger one for the teacher. In the corner stood a wood heater which provided more than adequate heat during the heavy winters. Damocles was sitting at his desk reading a book. He looked surprised to see her.

'Can you spare me a little of your time,' she asked, closing the door behind her.

'Of course, how can I be of help?

'This man — Eleftherios Venizelos, what can you tell me about him?'

Damocles snapped his book shut and looked at her with his piercing eyes.

'Hush,' he said in a low voice. 'Keep your voice down.'

Aspasia started to laugh. There was no-one else in the room.

He stood up and stalling for time to gather his thoughts, walked over to the heater to add a few more logs. Aspasia realised her presence made him uncomfortable and she decided to leave.

'I'm sorry. I didn't mean to intrude,' she said. 'Perhaps it was a bad idea to come here.'

Damocles poked the logs with a stick until a rush of red and orange flames began to shoot out of the grate.

'No,' he replied, wiping his hands. 'Please stay.'

'I appear to have embarrassed you. Is it that I am a woman here alone?'

'Not at all. This is a public building after all, and you have every right to be here.'

'Well what is it then?' Aspasia asked.

'Your question, Kyria Stavrides, it's not one that should be discussed openly.'

She looked quizzically at him. 'You are a man of learning and I am simply asking you about the Greek Prime Minister. What's wrong with that?'

'For me, nothing, but I fear that the mere mention of his name will ruffle a few feathers, especially now that we are at war with Greece.' He pulled up a chair beside her. 'Alright, I will tell you about him, but I want you to promise me that you will discuss this with no-one.'

Aspasia agreed.

'Have you heard of the *Megali Idea* — the Great idea?' Damocles asked.

Aspasia shook her head. 'No.'

'It's an idea that appeals to Greek intellectuals. In a nut-shell, it's about reclaiming the Hellenic lands of our ancestors in Western Asia Minor. You are aware that we Greeks were here long before the Turks, some say more three thousand years ago; at the very least since classical times.'

'Yes, I've visited some of the ancient sites and had the occasion to stumble across a section of a fallen temple whilst on my walks,' Aspasia replied, 'although I confess to knowing little about them.'

'The proponents of the *Megali Idea* believe this is where Hellenism flourished before it became an integral part of the Roman Empire. Because of the concentration of Greeks in Smyrna, Venizelos sees that city as the beating heart of this new Greek Empire and he believes that only the Christian population can take this idea forward. It is thought that there are some 800,000 Greeks in Smyrna alone and because they are well-educated, form the economic and intellectual backbone of this country.'

'And Constantinople?' Aspasia asked

'As the city of the Byzantine Empire, it signifies the greatness of its Christian past and will remain the seat of Orthodoxy. It is really Turkey's pre-Christian Hellenic traditions that are at the heart of the *Megali Idea*.'

Aspasia tried to digest Damocles' words. 'This man sounds very powerful. What does he look like?'

Damocles went to a bookshelf and took out two books. Inside were leaflets and cuttings from Greek newspapers. He handed them to her. One photograph of him in particular stood out. Venizelos was a broad-shouldered man and wore wire-rimmed spectacles and a pointed beard. It was his stature that struck Aspasia.

'He has a physical presence that commands attention,' she said. 'I can see why people would listen to him.'

'Some describe him as the greatest statesmen since Pericles,' Damocles replied. 'He is from a wealthy Cretan background and was christened Eleftherios the Liberator.'

Aspasia smiled. 'Christening a child with such a lofty title is a great burden for a young boy?'

'Not in his case. The whole family have been committed to the Greek cause for generations. Dying for his country is in his blood.'

Aspasia handed the papers back. 'And because of him, Christophorus might give his blood also,' she replied with more than a hint of sarcasm.

Damocles looked down at the floor. "I'm sorry. Sometimes it's better not to know these things.'

'I came here to be enlightened,' Aspasia said, quickly putting him at ease. 'The truth is not always what we want to hear. The point is, how many people here agree with him?'

Again, Damocles averted his eyes.

'Well? Does your silence mean that you also agree?'

For once, the normally eloquent Damocles was lost for words.

'I see,' Aspasia said. 'You *are* a follower then.' She leaned back in her chair and sighed heavily. 'You could be killed for this, you know.'

Damocles eyes flashed. 'Kyria Stavrides, I must remind you that it was you who came to me and I have been honest with you. Yes, I am a believer in this man. Asia Minor could be great again. You only have to look around you. Look at the Turks. Take your friend, Saniye, she is the same age as you but she can't even read or write. What hope has a race like that got?'

'I asked you how many Greeks here agree with him.'

Damocles waved his hand in the air. 'I can't tell you that,' he replied irritably. 'I wish I could. The groups operate in secret. The government has the secret police on the lookout for them. I have risked my neck telling you all this.'

'Your secret is safe with me, Damocles. I didn't come here to make trouble. I just want to understand a little about this damn war. That way, I can have an idea of Christophorus's fate.'

Aspasia thanked him for his time and handed him the biscuits, 'For your kindness. I baked them this morning. Can I come to you again?' she asked, 'if I have any more questions. I promise not to make a nuisance of myself.'

'Of course. I would like that.'

Outside, Aspasia was relieved to find the weather had cleared and she decided to go for a walk to the church to clear her head. There was much to think about. A man like Venizelos might be inspiring, but he was dangerous too. The Turks would not take very kindly to his idea of a Greater Greece and she feared a backlash. Where would it end?

CHAPTER 21

There is a God After All

Aspasia woke with the urge to vomit. The past few mornings had been the same but the feeling soon passed. This time she could not get out of bed in time and vomited over the side of the mattress. It was an unmistakable sign. She was pregnant. She fetched a cloth and a bowl of soapy water and, despite feeling ill, was so happy that she hummed a tune whilst she cleaned up the mess.

The last time she had lain with Christophorus was when he spent a few days at home, two weeks before he went away. Over the past few weeks, she knew something was not quite right with her body, but put it down to nerves due to him being away. She had also mentioned this to Saniye who was convinced she was with child.

'When did you last menstruate?' Saniye asked.

'Six weeks ago.'

'From what I can see, it's not nerves,' Saniye smiled. 'Your skin looks wonderful and your eyes sparkle.'

When Saniye told Ayşe Baci, her first reaction was that

Aspasia might miscarry again, so the old woman took it upon herself to prepare her special herbal tisanes. Every day before leaving the house to tend the goats, she placed a jug on the table for Saniye to take with her, and in the evening she waited anxiously for an update on Aspasia's health. When the time came for Aspasia to menstruate again, there was no sign of blood and the morning sickness continued. Mercifully, Ayşe Baci's secret concoctions had worked, and this time it seemed that she might actually carry the child to full term.

In light of recent events, Aspasia had begun to wonder if her payers were in vain. Now she was sure there was a God after all.

'Thank you, my sweet Virgin,' she murmured, as she kissed the silver icon. 'Thank you.'

After two more months, when her belly became rounder and her breasts more tender, she decided it was time to share the good news with her mother-in-law. Since her son had been called up, Kyria Stavrides had done nothing but grieve. Even her weaving suffered. She had always been a strong woman, but Christophorus's departure left a gaping hole, and it seemed that nothing could console her. They learnt from Ferit Ali that he had been deployed to Jerusalem with other Greeks. A carpet dealer who traded with The Anatolian Carpet Manufacturers Ltd. spotted him and wrote to tell of his plight. The letter was dated six weeks after Christophorus left Uşak.

My dear friend, Ferit Ali,
Last week I saw our good friend, Christophorus Efendi.
Can you imagine my surprise when I spotted this proud
man serving with a labour battalion? It grieves me to say
that he is one of many who have been reduced to cleaning

the streets and the removal of rubbish. He is in a pitiful state yet tries hard to maintain his dignity whilst others have been reduced to stealing and begging. With so little food about and disease rife, who can blame them? I have taken it upon myself to give him the odd food parcel, even though it is a dangerous thing for me to do. The authorities have little regard for the Christians and treat them no better than dogs. If we are found to be helping them we are taken out and hanged like common criminals.

This war has seen our economy collapse and the world we knew disintegrate around us. The depth of our moral degeneration knows no bounds. May Allah have mercy on our souls for what we have become.

Your friend,

Salim

Ferit Ali did not convey the heart of this letter to Aspasia, suffice to say that Christophorus was alive and under the watchful eye of a friend. Henceforth, both Kyria Stavrides and Aspasia could turn their attention to the pregnancy. It lifted their spirits and gave them cause for optimism. It was useless to think otherwise.

*

Throughout winter, Aspasia and Saniye worked on their carpet but they were in no hurry to finish. With Christophorus away and business almost at a standstill, who knew when someone would come from the factory to collect them? Aspasia was the only one who had wool left; enough for at least one more large carpet. In the evenings she returned to her embroidery. It

145

had always given her pleasure, and of late she had neglected it. There was plenty of red leather left over from Christophorus's document holder and she decided to make a folder in which to protect Sarah's beautiful carpet designs.

For the main design, she chose a central tree of life motif worked with thread over finely cut cardboard stencils, similar to the document holder. For the leaves and flowers, she would use a variety of stitches. At the base of the tree she left a space to embroider her name. Once the design was ready, she cut out the template and sorted through the threads that Christophorus had purchased for her on his trip to Bursa almost four years earlier. The yarns were so beautiful she had kept them aside for something special. Now that time had come. After this she would begin work on her unborn child's dowry — napkins, towels, cushions, etc.

She laid them out on the table in groups of colours, separating the soft delicate clouds of floss from the silk thread. On one side were the blues which ranged from the deepest indigo to the palest ocean wash. Next to these she laid out the green palette which she intended to use for the foliage: forest greens, moss and olive. On the other side were the yellows and oranges ranging from saffron and persimmon to butter. These blended well with her favourite palette — the warm reds with its varying shades of madder, rose and pomegranate.

There was also another, smaller group of browns and blacks: walnut and charcoal, and last of all a natural palette of white, ivory and cream. The blues Aspasia liked to blend with the silver threads, and the warmer yellow-red shades with the gold. The colours in her carpet were beautiful but nothing matched the ones for her embroidery. They were from natural dyes and pigments, and it gave her a great sense of satisfaction to work with them. After taking one colour from this palette, two from another and so on, Aspasia stood back and admired her final selection. She felt like a painter about to start work on a blank canvas.

Every now and again, Aspasia went to the school to visit Damocles. After her first visit, she wasn't sure if it was wise to know more about the war — after all, ignorance is bliss and she didn't want to jeopardise the pregnancy by worrying any more than could be helped. Yet the pregnancy also made her view things in a different light. She must be knowledgeable for her child's sake.

At least six weeks passed before she plucked up the courage to see Damocles again. On that visit, she learnt about the outbreak of the Russian Revolution and a man called Lenin. She also learnt about the fate of the Tsar and his family and that frightened her. If they could execute the Imperial Family there, then they might try to do it here with the Sultan's family. Damocles assured her that was not likely to happen as the Young Turk Revolution had already removed much of the Sultan's power.

'He is just a figurehead,' he told her.

A few weeks after that visit, Aspasia saw him again. This time she learnt about the Arab Revolt.

'But I thought the Arabs were Muslims,' she said with a puzzled expression, 'and therefore a part of the Holy War.'

'It seems not, Kyria Stavrides,' Damocles replied. 'The Allies have got in their ear and their propaganda is working. They want self-rule.'

Aspasia thought of Christophorus in Jerusalem.

'It's the best place for him,' Damocles added. 'A melting pot of religions: no-one is going to want unnecessary trouble in a city like that.'

On the first few visits, there was one subject Damocles purposely avoided but Aspasia's probing questions forced him to tell her.

'The Pontic Greeks around the Black Sea area have been forced from their homes,' he said. 'It seemed that they welcomed the Russians at the beginning of the war and now that the Bolshevik Revolution has caused the Russians to pull out of this war, they have been left high and dry. The Turks are making them pay dearly.'

'You mean like the Armenians?'

Damocles considered his words carefully. To tell her of their dire plight would not be wise, especially in her condition.

'I hear that many have fled to Greece,' was all that he would tell her.

CHAPTER 22

Aspasia's Gift

Springtime and early summer were always beautiful in Anatolia. The hardy winter crocuses, which came up in their thousands, were followed by blue muscari which carpeted the meadows like glorious sapphires on a silk carpet. It was as if God himself had taken a brush and painted the landscape with swathes of colour as far as the eye could see: white asphodels, bright yellow verbascum and pasqueflowers, red poppies, blue veronica the colour of the summer sky, and the spiny milk thistle with their pink-purple nodding heads. One cannot imagine how this splendorous sight lifted the spirits for the villagers of Stavrodromi and Pınarbaşı, even during war.

At the first sign of spring, the villagers started to plough their fields and the shepherds and goatherds took their animals out of the huts to find nourishment on the heavily pastured thorn-cushion vegetation that flourished on the treeless plateau after the winter snows melted. Ayşe Baci was one of them. This time she was accompanied by Cemal who travelled beside her on a donkey. It was a good sign that he was slowly returning

149

to his old self despite the fact that he would never fully recover from his injuries. Much of his rehabilitation was due to Ayşe Baci and Saniye's persistence. His mother's healing potions had the desired effect on both his body and mind, and the severe skin problems had healed completely although his eyesight had not yet fully recovered. Most heartening of all was that his state of mind had improved. For months he had refused to leave the house but with the arrival of spring he made an effort to venture further than the garden. With the aid of a good pair of crutches fashioned by the local carpenter, he was now able to make his way to the Coffee House of the Moon and the mosque with considerable ease.

But most of all, it was Saniye's unwavering love for him that gave him a new lease of life. When she wasn't weaving with Aspasia, she cooked his favourite meals and sat by his side as she did in the old days before Fatma arrived, and told him stories. Saniye might not have been able to read and write, but she was an imaginative storyteller and often told stories to Aspasia as they sat together weaving. Usually it was Turkish folktales; epics such as Dede Korkut. At other times it was about Nasreddin Hodja, and his antics made them laugh. She had even been known to recite poetry written by Süleyman the Magnificent. Occasionally Aspasia reciprocated and told her tales from the Iliad and the Odyssey, or Aesop's Fables, but she did not have Saniye's gift for mimicking the characters.

It was during one of these stories that Aspasia started to feel contractions.

'Bay Bichen Bey also rose and said: "Princes, pray for me too. Pray that Almighty Allah gives me a daughter." Saniye recited, not noticing Aspasia clutching her belly.

'The strong Oghuz princes raised their hands and prayed again saying, "May Almighty Allah give you a daughter.....'

At that moment Aspasia dropped her sharp carpet knife on the floor and stood up to get a glass of water.

Saniye jumped up immediately. 'Sit down, Sister. I will get it.'

Aspasia heard a soft popping noise and immediately felt a warm trickle of fluid running down her legs. Seconds later there was a stronger gush and she found herself standing in a puddle. Her waters had broken.

'Quickly,' she said to Saniye, 'fetch my mother-in-law.'

Saniye ran to Kyria Stavrides's house and banged on the door. Marika Stavrides did not have to ask what was wrong. She knew immediately. Next, Saniye went to the meydan to summon one of Ancient Yusuf's boys to fetch Ayşe Baci back from tending the goats on the plateau.

Throughout the day, Aspasia's contractions became more intense, but it was not until the middle of the night when her pains became unbearable and her screams could be heard throughout Stavrodromi. On the stroke of midnight, Aspasia gave birth to a healthy girl. The women gave thanks to God and said a few prayers to protect the child from the evil eye.

'A midnight child,' said Ayşe Baci. 'May the evil eyes stay away and may she bring you everlasting joy.'

Aspasia held the tiny bundle in her arms, the tears falling down her face.

'Light of my life,' she murmured softly, holding her tiny hand in hers. 'Your father will be so proud of you.'

'What are you going to call her?' asked Marika Stavrides.

'Elpida,' replied Aspasia. 'Hope. It's what we want most of all. Without it, we cannot carry on.'

The house saw a constant flurry of well-wishers and despite the scarcity of food there was always something to offer them. Between the joy that comes with a newborn and the novelty of the French clock, the house was christened "the house of good luck." Saniye and Marika Stavrides took it in turns to look after her and the child. One afternoon when Aspasia was sitting outside in the garden with the baby beside her, Saniye commented on the Tale of Bamsi Beyrik, Son of Kam Bure, the story she was telling Aspasia at the time her waters broke.

'Do you recall the story?' she asked.

'Of course,' Aspasia replied. 'The princes prayed for a daughter.'

Saniye smiled. 'Don't you see; it was an omen.'

Aspasia looked puzzled.

'In the old days, the prayers and curses of the princes were granted. Allah granted you your daughter.'

Aspasia didn't really see the relevance of the story, but she didn't want to upset her close friend who took things like this seriously.

'What else happened in the story,' she asked.

'Another prince also asked for a favour. He wanted a son.'

'And did Allah grant that son?' Aspasia asked, picking up Elpida and placing her next to her breast.

'Yes. What is more, the two families rejoiced and the children were engaged in the cradle.'

'What are you trying to say, Saniye?'

Saniye sat next to Aspasia as she breastfed the child and handed her an embroidered towel with which to wipe the excess milk.

'I am trying to tell you that I share Cemal's pillow again. He is not the lion of manliness he once was, but he is a lion nevertheless. The grief has been like hot oil burning away my breast and now the pain is gone. I see the joy Elpida brings to you and I wish the same.'

'I am happy for you both,' replied Aspasia, struggling for something to say. 'There's no reason why you shouldn't have children now. I will pray for you.'

Saniye stroked Elpida's forehead. 'You are something precious. Your lovely eyes shine like jewels,' she said in a soft voice. 'Let us hope that one day I will have a son and the two of you will marry. That day will be the happiest day of my life.'

Her words shocked Aspasia. 'My dear friend, you know as well as I do that such a union can never take place. What makes you say such a thing?'

'You always tell me the world is changing and we must change with it. You are like a sister to me. Surely you can see merit in what I propose. It will be the fruit of our friendship.'

Aspasia knew full well that Christophorus would never agree to such a thing, and neither did she for that matter. For the most part, the relationship between the Greeks and the Turks was harmonious, but mixed marriages were something both parties frowned upon. As for Cemal, the only way he would agree was on the condition Elpida converted, but that would never happen. Whilst the sentiment might have come with a kind heart, deep down, Aspasia wanted her child to prosper and that probably meant a life away from Stavrodromi. She had always felt that she had much in common with Saniye, but this comment made her realise that their worlds were quite different. All the same, Aspasia knew negative thoughts were not conducive for someone trying to become pregnant, so she decided to tread carefully for fear of upsetting her.

'I will pray for you,' she said. 'Have faith. You are a good woman and God will answer your prayers.'

'Will you light a candle for me in the Church of the Virgin?'

'I will do better than that,' Aspasia replied. She went inside and returned with her silver icon. 'The Holy Mother has looked after me, now she will look after you.'

'The day you give birth to a healthy child,' she said, deliberately omitting a gender, 'Is the day you can give it back to me.'

CHAPTER 23

A New Dawn

Hostilities between the Ottoman Empire and the Allies finally concluded with the signing of the armistice at Mudros Harbour on the island of Lemnos on 30th October 1918. The tentacles of war had reached into the farthest corners of the land and there was hardly a family who had not come through unscathed.

Aspasia put the final touches to her costume and checked herself in the mirror. She had retained her slim figure after giving birth and the joy of having Elpida in her life brought the sparkle back in her eyes again. *If only Christophorus would walk through that door, my happiness would be complete* she thought to herself, She picked up Elpida and joined the throng of villagers gathering in the meydan. This was the first time since Cemal's return that there had been cause for celebration. Festivities in the meydan were the lifeblood of the community, but the war had changed everything and it was obvious to everyone that the two villages were being torn apart. Whereas, previously both Greeks and Turks mingled, now there was a clear divide.

Aspasia sat next to Damocles.

'I fear things changed when Greece joined the war,' he said, in a low voice. 'They don't trust us any longer. The conditions laid out in the Peace Treaty haven't helped either. They are suffering the blackness of humiliation.'

Aspasia wondered if anyone there really understood the implications. She had a hard time understanding them herself. The musicians set up their chairs between the tables and started to play. The beautiful sound of the ney drifted through the warm evening air - restful, melancholic, yet filled with emotion. Aspasia's eyes filled with tears.

'I'm sorry,' she said, wiping her eyes. 'I don't know what came over me. Perhaps it's the uncertainty of everything.'

Soon, the ney was joined by the saz and the koltuk davulu, livening up the tempo. Under normal circumstances people would be dancing by now, but not tonight. Tassos came over and placed jugs of wine on the table, compliments of the Sun Coffee House.

'Our best dancers all went to war,' he said, setting down next to Aspasia and tucking into a plate of *yiouvetsi*. 'The rest are too old and the women won't dance with their men away. Our hearts are still bleeding. Perhaps things will be back to normal once they return.'

Damocles threw Aspasia a quick glance. Did he really believe that? War had touched them all. Over twenty men from Stavrodromi and Pınarbaşı had gone to war and as yet, only one had returned — Cemal.

*

156

It was still dark when Aspasia got up to rekindle the dying embers of last night's fire. She warmed her hands over the flames, and then checked on Elpida sleeping soundly in her bed before preparing biscuits to be cooked in the village oven. Outside, the village lay shrouded in a winter mist as thick as *fakes soupa*. The French clock chimed six o'clock. She had two hours to bake and clean the house before Saniye arrived. Today they were going to cut the carpet from the loom and finish the fringing.

Saniye arrived, rugged up in a thick coat with a woollen shawl wrapped tightly around her head and face with just enough space to see through.

'This weather chills me to the bones,' she said, shaking the dampness from the coat and scarf and laying them over a chair next to the hearth. 'How Cemal and my mother-in-law cope out there with the animals I will never know.'

Their voices woke Elpida, who started to cry. Saniye picked her up and gave her a cuddle and Elpida reciprocated by giving her a big smile. Saniye was like a second mother to her.

'Watch her for me, will you,' said Aspasia, picking up the tray of biscuits, 'while I take these to the oven. I won't be long.'

Aspasia headed up the street but the mist was so thick she could barely see in front of her. As she got closer, the aroma of baking filled the air. Several women were already there, huddled next to the hot oven while they waited for their food to cook. An old woman who lived next door was in charge. She took the tray from her, opened the heavy metal door with a stick and slid it inside next to other trays of biscuits, cakes and bread. At lunchtime, the oven would be re-filled with roasts and vegetable dishes. Firewood was still plentiful as everyone took it in turns to help collect the wood. Collecting wood for the village ovens was a fulltime job, and fortunately, one that was done throughout the year and not in such inclement weather as it was now.

The biscuits cooked in no time at all. Aspasia gave the old woman a few coins and returned to the house. When she turned into her street she saw a ghostly shape slowly walking towards her. At first it was hard to make out whether it was a man or woman as the person was heavily clothed and stooped badly. Then she saw it was a man in an army greatcoat. He looked up. Aspasia let out a scream and dropped the tray in shock.

'Christophorus!' she cried, running towards him. 'You're alive.'

The moment she threw her arms around him, his legs gave way and he collapsed to the ground. Her cry alerted the neighbours who came out to see what was going on. Saniye had just finished dressing Elpida, and was playing with her on the rug when she heard the commotion.

'Maşallah!' she cried, jumping to her feet. 'He's come back.'

Minutes later Christophorus was carried into the house by several old men. In no time at all, the word spread that he was home and the villagers arrived at the house to pay their respects.

'Put him there,' Aspasia said. 'On the divan next to the fire, and help him out of those clothes while I boil some water.'

When the men took of his greatcoat, Aspasia got the shock of her life. Christophorus was wearing the same clothes he wore the last time she saw him, only now they were filthy and tattered and several sizes too big. Elpida started to cry and Saniye took her into the next room. Seeing that they were undressing him, the other women departed. Removing his clothes was not easy, particularly the trousers, as they could not get his boots off. One of the men took his knife from his belt and started to cut them. Eventually, they removed them but the powerful stench of filth and rotting flesh combined with the cloying odour of stale urine and tobacco, filled the room and made them all retch.

Aspasia put the bowl on the floor next to him and started to sponge his face with warm soapy water.

'Get another bowl of water,' she said to the men, 'and wash his feet.'

At that moment Marika Stavrides entered the room. Seeing her son in such a pitiful state was too much for her, and she suffered such severe pains in her chest that Aspasia thought she was having a heart attack. But Marika Stavrides was made of sterner stuff and after the initial shock, quickly pulled herself together.

'Here, let me help,' she said.

Aspasia gave her the sponge and watched her clean her son's face as gently as if he were a child. In the meantime, she picked up the threadbare suit and threw it on the fire. The greatcoat was too bulky to burn and she threw that outside.

Watching her mother-in-law, clad in black and bent over her son, wiping his face and matted hair, Aspasia was reminded of images of the Virgin Mary tending Christ after the crucifixion that she had seen in the Roman Catholic Church in Uşak. Her grief was just as palpable.

Aspasia took over washing his feet. The abscesses and open wounds on his feet were worrying and even though the smell of decay was bad, his feet did not appear to be gangrenous. With care and Ayşe Baci's ointments, he would heal quickly. She wondered how on earth he had walked at all. Seeing that there was little more for them to do and happy in the knowledge that Christophorus was safe and sound, the visitors took their leave. Aspasia knew that others who had sent their sons to war had questions for him, but all that would have to wait.

Oblivious to all that was taking place, Christophorus fell into a deep sleep. When he woke, it was evening.

'Where am I?' he asked, clearly disoriented.

'You're home, my darling,' said Aspasia. 'Safe and sound.'

Their eyes locked. For a brief moment she wondered if he recognized her. He lifted his hand and touched her hair.

'Tell me it's not a dream,' he murmured.

'This isn't a dream, my beloved. You've come home.'

She helped him sit up and propped a cushion behind him whilst Marika ladled several large spoonfuls of *avgolemono* into a bowl.

'Eat this, my son. It will do you good.'

He ate slowly and then asked for more. It was a good sign.

The French clock chimed. He stared at it. Clearly it brought back memories of Sara.

'I never thought I would survive. You cannot imagine the conditions. They were unbearable.'

Aspasia squeezed his hand. 'You don't have to talk about it now.'

'I need to tell you. People must know what we've suffered. We were treated like animals. They didn't send us to fight like real men. Instead we were reduced to working like slaves. Every day there was another beating, another death. If you ran away you were shot. I would have died ages ago had it not been for our friend, Salim Efendi. He risked his life to give me food. At first

I worked in Jerusalem cleaning rubbish. If we didn't die of hunger and exhaustion, it was from disease. Then one day we were rounded up and sent to Damascus. We were huddled around a makeshift fire in a dilapidated building on the edge of the city when we heard the war had ended. We thought it was another one of their tricks to make us think we were free so that we would walk outside and give them an excuse to kill us. But when we saw the British Army, leading the defeated Ottoman soldiers through the streets, we knew it was true. My darling, I wept with joy. Fearing reprisals or that we should be taken for Turks, we stayed put until the building was searched by Allied soldiers. There were only seven of us: the rest perished. They kept us imprisoned for a few weeks. Salim Efendi found someone in Damascus to verify my identity and I was given the coat and told to go home.'

'How did you get here?' Aspasia asked.

'I managed to get a lift to Adana and then to Konya. From there I found a caravan train heading to Smyrna. The countryside is no longer safe, and they dropped me off not far from here.'

Aspasia told him that there were far less caravan trains coming through the village now. He wasn't surprised.

'The army requisitioned thousands of camels from the traders after sustaining losses in the attack on Suez alone - 7,000 from what I heard. What a disaster.'

At that moment, they heard a soft simpering noise coming from the next room. Aspasia exchanged glances with her mother-in-law.

What's that?' asked Christophorus. 'Is that a child?'

Aspasia got up quickly and disappeared into the next room. She scooped Elpida up in her arms and took her to him. His eyes widened in disbelief.

'Your child,' she said. 'She is the gift you gave me when we last slept together. I called her Elpida — Hope. We never gave up hope that you would return to us.'

Christophorus felt a lump rise in his throat. '*Christos kai Panagia*, Christ and the Virgin. This is a miracle.'

He put his hand out to touch her. 'Let me see her,' he said, barely able to utter the words.

Aspasia lowered Elpida, into his arms. Unsure who the stranger was, Elpida started to cry.

'She'll soon become accustomed to you.' Aspasia smiled, taking her back in her arms again. 'You are as much a shock to her as she is to you.'

The tears welled up in his eyes. 'This is the reason God allowed me to live,' he smiled.

*

Over the next few weeks, Aspasia's kitchen began to resemble Ayşe Baci's. Herbs of all descriptions hung in bunches from hooks along the wall, and an assortment of bottles and jars filled with everything from acrid smelling, viscous liquids to sweet-smelling scents infused with blossoms. Thankfully, Christophorus soon regained his health. Throughout this time there was a never-ending stream of visitors. One of the first was Ferit Ali who was eager to fill him in with news of The Anatolian Carpet Manufacturers Ltd.

'Thank goodness you've returned safe and well,' he said. 'It's been a terrible time. The carpet weaving ground to a standstill.'

'I can't wait to get back,' Christophorus replied. 'And put this war behind us.'

Ferit Ali assured him that his job was still there when he had fully recovered. For now he needed to regain his strength and spend time with his family. When he left, he took back the last two carpets Aspasia and Saniye had done.

'I've already found a home for these,' he smiled. 'The English in Constantinople: they will pay handsomely.'

The other visitor to the house was Damocles. He wanted to know if Christophorus had noticed any changes in the Christian community.'

'I was too busy trying to stay alive,' Christophorus replied, with more than a hint of sarcasm. 'The conditions were beyond description.'

Not long after Christophorus arrived home, two others returned from the war. Ömer, the Turkish grocer's son, and another Turk from Pınarbaşı, a man called Mustafa who had joined up of his own free will in the early days of the war. Nikos, Ilyias and Mikis, the three shepherds, Tassos's son, Thanassos, and Vassilis, the grocer's son, all disappeared without a trace. The loss of Thanassos and Vassilis in particular, shook Aspasia and Christophorus.

Of the Turks who failed to return, most families received notification that they were killed in action. Almost three million conscripts and officers had been mobilized and twenty-five percent of the population perished, more from disease than in battle. Everywhere, families were left with only the elderly, children and young widows. Combined with serious food shortages and famine in the east, social disintegration was inevitable. Stavrodromi and Pınarbaşı were no exception.

CHAPTER 24

The Occupation of Smyrna

Ferit Ali caught Sotiris Lambros's eye and he ordered another bottle of French wine.

'I can't tell you how much I've thought about this place,' Christophorus said, finishing his evening meal. 'It seems years since we were last here.'

He looked around the dining room. It was just as he remembered it, filled with happy customers and a lively band playing the latest music. There were even a few couples on the dance floor.

'Sotiris did a good job under the circumstances,' Ferit Ali said. 'Thankfully, the officers who stayed here were of a better class of people and not given to drunkenness and theft, which seemed to be a common occurrence elsewhere.'

Sotiris brought over the wine and opened it for them. 'Good to have you back again, Christophorus. I hear you are now the proud father of a beautiful girl.'

Christophorus's eyes lit up. 'She is almost one year old. My wife has brought her to Uşak. They will be staying with her

165

family for a few days. I want her to buy a few new clothes, and we will have our first family photograph taken.'

'That's good to hear,' Sotiris replied. 'It makes a change to see our womenfolk going about their business again. Very few ventured out when the war was on, you know. And there was nothing to buy anyway. The shops were empty.'

He called a waiter over and asked him to bring a platter of dried fruit, courtesy of the management.

'I am afraid desserts are not as fanciful as before the war.'

'Believe me, after what I've been through, this is a banquet,' Christophorus smiled. 'I am savouring every mouthful.'

Sotiris put his hand on his shoulder and wished him well.

Ferit Ali took a sip of wine. 'Now our stomachs are nicely satisfied. Let's get back to business. Where was I?'

'The carpets that have gone to Constantinople,' Christophorus replied. 'Did they fetch a good price?'

'Excellent, especially Aspasia's, but we are in dire need of more wool. See what you can get from your contacts. Do you have enough for your mother and Aspasia?'

'Enough for one more, but I am afraid they don't have much time these days. Elpida needs attention and my mother is slowing down. The worry of me being away has taken its toll on her. He paused for a moment. 'You know my dear, Ferit Ali, I owe you so much. The money you gave us saved us. Aspasia told me how foodstuff was hard to come by, and what she could get was at inflated prices; not to mention the bribes I paid out for my own survival. I hate to think what would have happened if we had not had it.'

'You are not only a loyal man, Christophorus; you are like a son to me.'

All the same, I owe you my life.'

'Let us drink to the future,' Ferit Ali said, picking up his glass. 'Here's to success again.'

'To success — and happiness,' replied Christophorus.

*

The photographic studio in Uşak was run by Constantine Theotakis, one of two brothers who started their business in Smyrna some twenty years earlier. Whilst the Smyrna studio catered for the fashionable elite and did a roaring business, even through the war, Constantine's business focused more on trade. The Oriental Carpet Manufacturers Ltd. was their main customer, as the catalogues constantly needed updating. Ferit Ali and Christophorus had looked after Constantine in the past, so Constantine was more than delighted to take a Stavrides family portrait.

The spacious studio was filled with backdrops of varying images, from archaeological columns set in bucolic landscapes, to richly decorated interiors. Aspasia chose the interior setting and was given a choice of chairs, tables and carpets.

In no time at all, everything was neatly assembled and the pair positioned themselves in readiness for their first family portrait. Aspasia had decided against wearing her traditional costume and instead chose a European-style silk gown purchased the day before in Uşak's only department store. Made out of flowing, pale green silk, it was fastened at the waist with a dark green velvet band. To compliment the effect, she combed her hair up in a soft roll, and wore a matching velvet choker which emphasised her elegant neck to perfection. On her feet, she wore her favourite slippers, the cream silk ones that Christophorus had bought her in Bursa. Her eyes sparkled with happiness.

Constantine seated her on a high-backed chair with Christophorus standing behind her. Elpida, dressed in a cream frilly dress with a matching bonnet, sat on her mother's lap playing with a rag doll that Christophorus had given her. After a few adjustments, Constantine put his head under the black cloth and looked through the view-finder whilst giving them instructions on where to look. Seconds later there a bright flash.

'Excellent,' Constantine declared. 'I think you will be very happy with the results.'

Aspasia removed her cream slippers and put them back in her bag. This was the first time she had worn them outside their home and she didn't want them to get dirty. Christophorus slipped a shawl over her shoulder and whispered something in her ear. She blushed. It had been a long time since they were as carefree as this. They were about to depart when an assistant called Constantine out of the room saying he had something urgent to tell him and it couldn't wait. He excused himself for a minute leaving Aspasia and Christophorus alone. Christophorus took Elpida and gave her a kiss on the cheek.

'The next time you have your photograph taken, my precious one,' he said with a smile, 'You will have a little brother or sister with you.'

Moments later, an ashen-faced Constantine returned to the room.

'What on earth's happened?' Christophorus asked.

'We've just received word that the Hellenic Army has landed in Smyrna.'

Recalling Damocles's words about Venizelos's *Great Idea*, Aspasia shot Christophorus a quick glance and instinctively reached for his arm.

'You're sure about this?' Christophorus said. 'It's not a rumour?'

Constantine shook his head. 'This is no rumour, my friend. They have landed and taken over the Konak. Already there are riots breaking out.'

Outside the atelier, the street was beginning to fill with people, all eager to learn more. Christophorus took Elpida from Aspasia and they headed to the Hotel Europa. In a scene, reminiscent of the days when war broke out, a crowd gathered at the reception clamouring for news.

'It's true,' Sotiris said to them. 'The Greeks have occupied Smyrna and Metropolitan Chrysostomos has welcomed them.' He waved his hands in the air trying to calm everyone down.

'It's only to restore order until things get sorted out,' he shouted out over the noise.

There were jeers and shouts from some of the Turks in the lobby.

'Damn that Venizelos. May he rot in hell,' someone cried out in Turkish.

A scuffle broke out and a Greek was set upon by a Turk.

'That's enough!' shouted Sotiris, 'before I have you all put in jail for disturbing the peace. I will not tolerate such behaviour in my establishment.'

'You'd better get back to Stavrodromi,' Christophorus said to Aspasia, 'until all this is sorted out. It will be quieter there.'

'I won't leave you,' Aspasia replied. 'Not again. We have to stick together.'

'What about my mother? We can't leave her alone. She will be worried sick?'

Aspasia thought it over. 'Alright,' she answered reluctantly, 'but only if you promise to return every week as you used to. We need you.'

Christophorus returned to the factory while Aspasia went to fetch her things. Ferit Ali was pacing his office waiting for him.

'*Boku yedik!*' he said angrily. 'We're done!' How much more can we take?'

'Ferit Ali, I must go back to Stavrodromi with Aspasia. I don't like her travelling alone. I will be back straight away.'

Ferit Ali stared at him. 'You Greeks will be the death of us,' he shouted, waving his fists at Christophorus. 'Go if you must, but if you fail to return after one week, I will replace you. Do you hear?'

Christophorus was lost for words. Was his superior telling him that he didn't trust him anymore? Surely not. Only a few days ago he was telling him he was like a son. Everything had been fine until now. He moved closer to him as if to assure him he was not one of those Greeks who welcomed this move.

'One week, Christophorus,' Ferit Ali said. 'One week.'

*

Given the situation, no-one wanted to travel alone. There was safety in numbers and so Christophorus and Aspasia joined several more families returning to their villages. It was mid afternoon when they arrived in the meydan and it was deserted. Christophorus gave Ancient Yusuf's boys a coin each to escort

Aspasia home and carry their bags whilst he settled his horse in the caravanserai. Ancient Yusuf was sitting in his usual place, finishing a plate of wheat and *pekmez*.

'Terrible business,' he said to Christophorus, putting his plate on the ground to attend to the horse.

Christophorus didn't need to ask what business he was talking about. News travelled slowly through the backwaters of Anatolia, but in this case, it spread with the speed of a wild fire. He felt embarrassed, as though he was forced to justify his position on the situation.

'It has nothing to do with us here,' he replied, defensively.

Ancient Yusuf stroked the horse. He had a way with animals.

'Maybe, maybe not. We'll see.'

There was something cold and sinister about his reply, but it was pointless to argue, so Christophorus let it pass. Before going home, he decided to call in at the Sun Coffee House. Damocles was sitting by the open window drinking tea with Tassos.

'Mind if I join you?' he asked and took a seat while Tassos refilled the samovar. 'Well, Damocles, your prediction about the Greeks was right after all. Looks like Venizelos got his way.'

'A new beginning,' Damocles replied.

'Or the beginning of the end,' said Christophorus, sarcastically.

Damocles smiled. 'We Greeks will benefit from this union, mark my words.'

'And the Turks?'

'The Turks will not suffer. No-one wants that. A whole new world will open up for them. Venizelos will see to it that every-one will be better off. He will implement more schools and give them an education. Look at the Turks in Pınarbaşı. Hardly any of them can read or write. It's pitiful.'

Christophorus was beginning to get angry.

'So all the time you were educating my wife, you were really hoping she would come round to your way of thinking.'

'You can't change progress, my friend. The Allies won the war. They have the upper hand.'

'My job is on the line because of all this,' Christophorus replied, angrily. 'My boss, who has supported me through thick and thin — a Turk, I might remind you, who has also helped support the weavers and spinners of these villages — now views me with suspicion. Have you any idea how that makes me feel?'

'Steady, you two,' said Tassos, placing the tea on the table. 'Don't let's quarrel between ourselves. What's done is done. We've got problems of our own here, without you two adding to them.'

'What do you mean?' asked Christophorus, trying to calm down.

'This morning, Hasan asked me to join him for breakfast in the Coffee House of the Moon. Imam Süleyman was with him. It seems that three Turks left the village before daybreak to join Mustafa Kemal's Nationalists.'

Christophorus slammed his glass down so hard, the tea spilt on his trousers.

'You see,' he said to Damocles, his voice rising again. 'The first signs of resistance.' He got up to leave. 'Now our own have deserted us.'

'They're not exactly our own,' Damocles replied. 'They're Turks. Since when have we been one of them? We don't even allow each other to intermarry — unless it's on their terms.'

Christophorus clenched his fist as if to strike him.

'Idiot! You sit behind a desk and fill your head with nonsense, but I was the one who was forced in to the war. I saw their disillusionment first hand. Kemal will have them eating out of the palm of his hand. They died for him at Gallipoli; they will die for him again.'

Tassos pulled his arm. 'Christophorus, calm down.'

'And another thing,' Christophorus added, wagging his finger at Damocles. 'We have grown up with them. They are our brothers.'

With that he stormed outside and marched home. Aspasia was with her mother-in-law when they heard the door slam.

'What on earth's the matter?' she asked.

'What started as a good week has ended in disaster, that's what.'

'So you heard about the three Turks then?' Marika Stavrides said, matter-of-factly.

'What three Turks?' Aspasia asked, looking anxiously from one to another.

Her mother-in-law told her the same story. One of them was Ömer, the grocer's son.

'Now you know why I am in a filthy mood, 'Christophorus said. 'All this could have been avoided.'

CHAPTER 25

Pandora's Box

Christophorus stayed in Stavrodromi for a few more days and then returned to Uşak. He avoided Ferit Ali as much as possible until he was in a better mood, while spending most of his time sorting out the wool supplies and interviewing new weavers. Within a couple of months, the situation more or less returned to normal and Christophorus heaved a sigh of relief when Ferit Ali invited him to dinner at the Hotel Europa. If he hoped the old days were returning, he was wrong. Uşak was now filled with foreign journalists again and they made good use of their information which wasn't good.

It soon became common knowledge that the town of Aydin, south of Smyrna, had seen unprecedented unrest. The Turks were not happy at the Greek army landing in Smyrna and had gone on a rampage, plundering public buildings, destroying machinery, burning much of the Greek Quarter to the ground and hunting the local Greeks like rats. Within days, reinforcements arrived from Smyrna and the devastating acts of reprisals started all over again. Most Turks fled. Similar scenes were taking place elsewhere and the Greek army was forced further afield into Anatolia. In August 1920, the Greek army entered Uşak and Bursa. Uşak was now a Greek garrison.

Ferit Ali remained cool but withdrawn. The lines of business were open again and his thoughts were on establishing trade again rather than war. The new weavers were coming along nicely and he had Christophorus to thank for that. The one change he did make was that henceforth, all carpets would only be made in the factories. It was deemed far too dangerous to send agents into the countryside. The village weavers would just have to rely on their own resources and if any finished a carpet, they were to bring it to Uşak themselves. With stocks of wool at an all time low, Christophorus took a trip to Bursa. The Greek presence was everywhere.

He went to catch up with Nurettin at his Kebab House and was told that he was no longer in Bursa. At first his father-in-law, who now ran the business, refused to say where he was, but seeing that Christophorus would not let up, he was told that he had gone to join Mustafa Kemal's Nationalists.

'I am sorry, my friend,' the man said. 'The occupation of Bursa has sent us into deep mourning. It will not end until the Greeks have left our soil.'

The two friends were now firmly on opposite sides of the political divide.

Dejected, Christophorus made his way to Davit Sarkissian's shop. It was now owned by a Turk. No-one had any idea where the Sarkissian family had gone to. All this was reported to Ferit Ali who simply shrugged. Kemal's Nationalist's were not sanctioned by the government in Constantinople, yet it appeared that anyone with an ounce of fighting spirit was scurrying off to join up. The war had opened a Pandora's Box and the Nationalist cause was on the ascent.

*

Aspasia was at the village oven when she heard the commotion.

'The Greeks,' someone shouted out. 'The Greek army is here.'

She scooped Elpida in her arms and followed everyone else to the meydan. The Greek army had already filled the area with trucks, carts and horses. A short, stocky man with a rugged dark complexion and a thick moustache appeared to be their commander and was ordering troops to search the neighbourhood. They wasted no time in running through the area knocking on all doors and ordering everyone to gather in the meydan. The coffee houses had been filled with old men when the Greek army entered and all, including the owners were told to step outside. The commander asked for a table to be set up in the square. Damocles helped Tassos bring one out from the Sun Coffee House, and they set it up under the shade of a plane tree. Tassos then ran back and made the officer a cup of coffee and placed it on the table. No thanks were offered.

When it appeared that everyone had gathered together, the commander wanted everyone's name, religion, address and occupation. Anyone caught lying would be shot without question. The summer sun was beating down fiercely and Aspasia thought she would faint if she stood there much longer. When everyone's details were duly written down, the inhabitants of Stavrodromi and Pınarbaşı were segregated, either to the right or the left, depending on their religion. Five people including Ayşe

Baci and Cemal were missing; shepherds and goatherds, who were still on the plateau. A group of soldiers were sent to fetch them. An hour later, they all returned. Aspasia gave Elpida to her mother-in-law who shaded the child's head with her shawl. The child was two years old now and restless. She wanted to be put down, but the women were afraid she would try to run away and attract unwanted attention. Marika Stavrides soothed her gently and handed her nuts which she always kept in her skirt pocket.

Soon everyone was dismissed until further notice. The commander ordered Ancient Yusuf and his boys to look after the animals. There was one last order. No-one was to leave the village without prior approval. Soldiers were posted at the entrances to the villages.

'We will be setting up camp here for a while,' the commander said. 'It would pay you all to be civil and no harm will come to any of you.'

With that, the villagers were dismissed and the commander and a lieutenant went to the Sun Coffee House for refreshments. Hasan's Coffee House of the Moon was out of bounds to the soldiers. Aspasia gave Elpida to her mother-in-law and went back to the oven to retrieve her partly charred dish of stuffed roast peppers and tomatoes.

'Stay at my house,' Aspasia said to her mother-in-law. 'I don't want you going home alone now.'

By sunset, Elpida was asleep in her mother's bed as Aspasia and Marika settled down to eat. It was the time of the day that Aspasia enjoyed the most. A peaceful and tranquil time, but tonight a dark cloud hung over the villages. The pair almost jumped out of their skin when they heard a knock at the door. It was Damocles.

Aspasia let him in and bolted the door after him.

'I've just had a meeting with the commander,' he said. 'They have asked if there are any houses they might requisition. I thought of you.'

Aspasia grew angry. 'Oh you did, did you? A woman all alone! I thought better of you than that.'

'Let me finish, please, Kyria Stavrides. The commander only wanted one or two. The rest have set up tents in the valley. He made it clear that whoever was accommodating would get extra rations. I have given over the school room to some of them. I thought that perhaps your mother-in-law might give up her home and move in with you for a while — just until they move on of course. I am sure the commander would look kindly on you for this.'

'You impudent man!' shouted Marika.

Damocles turned to leave.

'Wait,' Aspasia said. 'It is worth thinking about. Christophorus would also want you here with us now. And it might pay to be on their good side.'

Damocles smiled. 'I thought you would see merit in the idea.'

'When is this to take place?'

'Tomorrow morning.'

'Fine. Tell him we agree, but he is to treat the place with respect,' Aspasia added.

'He is the commander. Of course he will be courteous.'

Aspasia and her mother-in-law were not aware of the atrocities that had taken place since the Greek occupation. They just prayed things would stay calm.

After Damocles left, Marika slumped back in her seat and

pushed her plate of vegetables away. 'I've lost my appetite,' she said miserably.

Aspasia wished Christophorus was home. Perhaps she had been wrong after all in wanting to return to Stavrodromi. They should all have gone to Uşak.

The following day, the commander and his adjutant moved into Marika's house, She packed a few of her prized possessions and moved in with Aspasia. She was also given a sack of wheat and beans as thanks. Later that evening, a raucous revelry of drinking took place in Marika's house and the noise carried along the street and over the rooftops. Aspasia bolted the door. Sometime around midnight, the noise stopped. Maybe now they could get some sleep. It was not to be.

Screams pierced the warm night air. The soldiers were carrying out house to house searches in the Turkish quarter. Aspasia shuddered.

'Holy mother of God! What are they doing? I am afraid for Saniye and Ayşe Baci.'

'There's nothing we can do until daybreak,' replied her mother-in-law. 'We must stay put.'

Hours later, they could smell burning coming from the area of Pınarbaşı. The women huddled together, shaking like leaves.

At the first light of dawn, the inhabitants of both villages were called to the meydan again. It was then that they saw the charred ruin of the mosque half way up the main street of Pınarbaşı. The commander, pacing up and down in front of his make-shift desk, was in a filthy mood.

'Last night my men carried out raids and this is what we found,' he said, pointing to a small mound of guns and knives on the floor. 'It is common knowledge that the Nationalists have their spies everywhere and are waiting to strike. Do you want to see what happens to those who are suspected of such crimes?'

The villagers shifted uncomfortably as two elderly Turks were pushed forward and forced to kneel in front of him. Their legs shook like leaves in an autumn wind and they begged for mercy saying that the guns were old and had not been fired for ages. They were merely family keepsakes.

The commander picked one up. It was an ornate, silver flintlock pistol probably made before 1900. He looked at it carefully and then put it on his desk. The others were equally as old and useless — except for one — a Mannliche semi-automatic pistol of the type used in the Balkan wars and the Great War. He pointed it at one of the old men.

'Who did you intend to use this on?' he asked, twisting his thick moustache with his free hand.

An officer translated.

The man was in tears. 'No-one: it was given to me after the war.'

The commander pointed in the direction of the mosque, now a charred ruin, and asked Imam Süleyman to step forward.

'These men are your flock. Which one is to die because they have violated the rules?'

The villagers looked at each other. What rules? The only rules about keeping weapons applied to the Christians.

'These men have done no wrong,' Imam Süleyman replied, defiantly. 'Shoot me rather than them if you must. And let us live in peace.'

The commander took his own gun out of his holster, aimed it at the Imam's head and cocked the trigger. Unafraid of death, the Imam stared defiantly at him. In the next second, the commander turned the pistol on the old man he had questioned, and shot him in the head instead. A spurt of red gushed from his head and he slumped forward to the screams of the women in the crowd, two of whom, passed out. The children started to cry, including Elpida who had no idea what was going on but sensed her mother's terror. Aspasia quickly turned Elpida's head, pushing her face into her skirt and almost suffocating her. Elpida struggled but Aspasia held her tightly.

The commander called Ancient Yusuf and his two boys over. 'Get rid of him,' he ordered.

Then he turned to the crowd. 'Let that be a lesson to you. The Greek army is in command here. Now go about your business.'

With that he marched off. Ancient Yusuf's two boys could barely move, they were in such a state of shock. A sack was thrown over the body and it was removed to the han to be prepared for burial. Saniye, her mother-in-law, and Cemal, had also been present, but they refused to look across at Aspasia. When the crowd started to disperse, Aspasia gave Elpida to her mother-in-law and ran to catch up with them.

'It's best if you stay away, Sister,' Saniye whispered. 'It's not good for us to be seen together.'

Aspasia refused to accept that.

'Meet me at the Church of the Virgin this afternoon, during the siesta.'

Saniye nodded and hurried on.

At two-thirty in the afternoon, Aspasia made her way to the church. The village was bathed in an eerie silence and the smell of burning still hung in the air. Aspasia pushed open the church door. Saniye was waiting for her by the candles.

'What happened last night?' Aspasia asked.

'The soldiers decided to do midnight raids. If we didn't open up, they broke the doors down. We were all in bed, but they had no regard for the women. Even I was poked and prodded — leered at like an animal in the market. It was sickening. Cemal protested but they hit him with a rifle and threatened to shoot him. When they found those guns, all hell broke loose and they targeted the mosque.' Saniye began to cry. 'It was so old — a part of the landscape. Now it's gone, and we have no money to build another.'

Aspasia hugged her friend tightly.

'I am afraid to come and see you,' Saniye said, wiping her eyes. 'I don't want to provoke them. We've heard rumours that the soldiers in the next village treated the Turks appallingly. They even raped the women.' She started to cry again.

'Hush, my friend. I'll see what I can do.'

Saniye gave a sad smile. 'You are powerless, Aspasia. Even Christophorus would be powerless too, were he here. We just have to pray it will be over soon.'

The women sat on the church wall overlooking the village for a while. Here and there, a stork's nest clung precariously on top of several rooftops. From this vantage point, they had a clear view of the blackened mosque. Not a soul could be seen in the Turkish Quarter, and the narrow valley that snaked out of the villages to the plateau was filled with tents. In the meydan, they could make out the commander at his desk surrounded by several soldiers. Aspasia thought of the times she and Saniye had sat on this same wall discussing Fatma. How long ago it all seemed now.

'What a nightmare,' Saniye said despondently.

*

Aspasia walked up to the commander, seated at his desk tapping away on his typewriter, and asked for a moment of his time. Another officer got up and offered her his chair.

'What can I do for you, Kyria?' he asked.

'I am the daughter-in-law of Kyria Stavrides whose house you now occupy. I need to discuss something with you. You may or may not know that Stavrodromi and Pınarbaşı are important carpet weaving villages. What I am trying to say is that your presence is frightening some of the weavers, particularly the Turkish ones, and I am afraid the weaving will suffer.'

The commander studied her carefully.

'What do you expect me to do about that?'

'Well, I would like them to know that your men will not hinder them going about their business. For instance, I work on special pieces with a Turkish lady, Saniye, and she is afraid to come to my house. It means that our weaving is behind. The factory in Uşak pays us and we need that money.'

'Which factory is that?'

Aspasia could see he was ready to listen.

The Anatolian Carpet Manufacturers Ltd. My husband is a manager there. He gives us work. Many of our carpets are sold overseas. Some even in Greece.'

'Where does this Saniye live?' he asked.

Aspasia gave him the address. The commandant clicked his fingers and a soldier jumped to attention.

'Go and find this woman,' he said. 'And bring her here immediately.'

The soldier saluted and accompanied by a couple of other soldiers, they ran to Saniye's house. She was preparing a meal when they banged on the door. Her mother-in-law and Cemal were out with the goats. Nervously, she peered out of the window and panicked when she saw who it was. There was no escape; she had to open the door.

'What can I do for you?' she asked, wringing her hands together frantically.

'You are to come with us to the meydan immediately.'

Saniye immediately thought of Cemal. Had he done something foolish against the Greeks as he often threatened to do? Was she being punished because he hated them so much? Her fears eased when she saw Aspasia with the commander.

'Saniye, wife of Cemal, the goatherd,' the commander said. 'This lady tells me you are a carpet weaver?'

'Yes, sir,' Saniye stammered.'

'And you work together?'

'That's correct.'

'Then please continue. I don't want you to be afraid. You may come and go to this lady's house as you wish. In fact, we will all go there together right now, and you can show me what you do.'

Aspasia was stunned. This man who had just shot someone in cold blood was acting extraordinarily courteously and it threw her.

'It will be our pleasure, Sir.'

The two women walked ahead with the commander and his entourage close behind. When they entered the house, Marika

Stavrides was sitting on the divan sewing. At the sight of the commander she pricked her finger in shock, causing droplets of blood to fall on to the cloth.

'The gentlemen have come to see our fine work, mama,' Aspasia said, quickly putting her mother-in-law at ease.

Marika sat in silence, pressing her finger hard to stem the blood, as Aspasia showed them the large loom and a half-finished carpet.

'This is it,' she said. 'The design was given to me by the factory's chief designer.'

The commander ran his thick fingers across the pile and studied it. He was clearly impressed, commenting favourably on the sharp colours and closeness of the weave. Aspasia added that if he was still here when it was finished, the factory might consider giving it to him as a gift. The commander smiled.

'We will see,' he replied. Then he shot a glance towards Saniye. 'Be thankful these people are looking after you.'

The French Clock chimed six o'clock, amusing the commander and his entourage and lightening the atmosphere. Aspasia told him it was a gift from the factory for their work. After he left, the women all breathed a sigh of relief.

'From now on,' Aspasia said to Saniye. 'Try and spend as much time here as possible. It's safer.'

Saniye kissed Aspasia and her mother-in-law's hands and burst into tears again.

'How can I ever thank you, Sister? I will pray for you.'

CHAPTER 26

The Summer Offensive

All remained relatively peaceful in Stavrodromi and Pınarbaşı until the summer of the following year. The Greek army had expanded its territory, but it was tenuous. Many Turks were fleeing to join the Nationalists. Christophorus came home several times, and because business had picked up and the money flowed once more, stayed longer, sometimes for a week at a time. The commander was still in charge and Christophorus promised him the factory would be honoured to present him with Aspasia and Saniye's carpet as a gift for maintaining the peace. The carpet was coming along nicely, but at a much slower pace than normal. No-one wanted to give it to a man who had killed one of their own in such a callous manner. They didn't trust him. Instead, much of the two women's time was spent embroidering. Elpida had just had her third birthday. She was a beautiful child with dark curly hair and large eyes framed by long silky lashes. Everyone doted on her, especially her papa, who brought her presents every time he visited. By now, Aspasia and Christophorus had hoped for a brother or sister for their pride and joy, but as yet it was not to be.

At the end of June, the villagers couldn't help noticing a renewed scurry of activity. The commander came to see them one day to say that he and his men were moving on. He wouldn't tell them where. He added that he was sorry the carpet wasn't finished as he was sure his wife would have loved it. The soldiers departed the next day, but were soon followed by others. Fortunately, these new arrivals passed through the villages without causing havoc.

For two months, a steady convoy of vehicles and mule trains passed through the village and the coffee houses did a roaring trade. Even Hasan was not averse to serving the Greek soldiers, though many didn't bother to pay. Aspasia and Saniye heaved a sigh of relief that the beautiful carpet would not end up in the hands of the commander. Still, they decided against finishing it, just in case he did return.

The week after the army moved on, Christophorus returned and his mother moved back into her own home.

'What a trying time,' Aspasia said to him. 'Do you realise how long it's been since we were alone. I mean truly alone.'

Christophorus pulled her to him and smothered her face with kisses. 'I love you for taking care of mama. I could not wish for a more considerate and loving wife.'

Aspasia whispered coquettishly in his ear. 'Elpida is sleeping. Let's go and lie under the loquat tree and make love as we used to do.'

Christophorus smiled, picked her up in his arms and took her into the garden. It was moments like this that had sustained him over the past few years. How he wished these moments would last forever.

Troop movements through and near the villages carried on for a couple of months. Some days there would be long columns, at other times it would be peaceful. Those were the days the villagers congregated around the fountain spending their time in idle chatter. In August, it soon became clear that something important was taking place. On August 23, the summer offensive began with the Battle of Sakarya. The river Sakarya, east of Ayfon and Eskişehir, looped through a parched landscape of some of the most inhospitable country the Greeks had yet encountered. It was deemed important to conquer because from there, they could take Ankara, the seat of Kemal's Nationalists. The clinging sand and dirt caused breakdowns, and the logistics of transporting weapons to the front, plus carrying water and food, became a nightmare. The Greeks fought valiantly along a front of sixty miles and at one point, it seemed that they might break the Turkish lines, but it was not to be. On September 11, sensing the Greeks were tired and weary, Kemal ordered a counterattack. 100,000 Greeks pitted themselves against 90,000 Turks. The hillsides and trenches lay covered in bodies. Thousands of Greeks were taken prisoners with at least another 20,000 casualties. Any hope of the Greeks occupying Asia Minor was now gone. In a humiliating retreat, bridges were blown up and abandoned villages destroyed or set on fire. The Greeks were exhausted and they were disillusioned.

Aspasia was leaving the Church of the Virgin when she recognised the tell-tale signs of a long cloud of dust in the distance. The soldiers were returning. She ran towards the village to warn Saniye, telling her to pack a few things and make haste to her home for safety. Then she alerted others. Hasan closed his coffee house and ran home to his family. Even before their arrival, word had spread of a Greek defeat. Fear and panic was palpable.

Two hours later, the meydan was filled with broken-down, dust-clogged vehicles, pack animals and soldiers. Tired and hungry, they were also angry. Someone had to pay. The Turks were ripe for the picking. At sunset, some of them went on a rampage, but unlike last time, their rage made them lose reason. The houses in Pınarbaşı were broken into, men women and children were slaughtered indiscriminately in their homes or chased through the streets, only to be callously murdered when they were caught. Several women were raped before being mutilated, and their screams carried through the air like sirens in the night. Saniye cowered behind Aspasia's bedroom door in a foetal position with her hands over her ears, sobbing uncontrollably. Elpida thought she was playing a new game and kept pulling at her skirt until Aspasia grabbed her and pulled her away.

In the morning, the soldiers moved on, leaving behind the ravages of war. All the Turkish houses had been looted and bodies lay strewn in the alleyways or in their homes. Rudimentary furniture that had been handed down as dowry pieces lay broken and smashed in an orgy of anger. Several houses were on fire. If there was ever a hell on earth, then this was it. It was going to be another hot day and already the cloying stench of death permeated the air. Even the fragrance of the blossoms and trees could not hide it.

After the fires were extinguished and the bodies were all accounted for, it appeared that some had managed to flee into the hillside. Amongst the dead were six children and ten women, one of whom was pregnant, and at least half the men of Pınarbaşı. Hasan's coffee house stood in ruins, but thankfully his body was not amongst the dead. The villages of Stavrodromi and Pınarbaşı would never be the same again.

Saniye was in hysterics when she saw what had happened, pacing the street and banging her head with the palms of her hand.

'Curse this village,' she wailed. 'Curse everyone.'

Mercifully, Cemal and his mother were not at home when it happened, and she had no idea where they were. The village was in deep shock. The Greeks tried their best to comfort their neighbours. They offered food and shelter, and made promises to help rebuild the village. But nothing could replace the dead, and rebuilding the trust would take generations. This was a land of long memories and vendettas.

*

Of the Turks who fled the village, only five returned. Cemal and Ayşe Baci, who saw what was happening on their way back from herding the goats, took refuge amongst the rocks. With them was an old shepherd, Imam Süleyman, and Hasan. Others, who had managed to escape the wrath of the Greek soldiers, fled the village for good. The Nationalists needed to do very little now to expand their base and their numbers swelled at an alarming rate.

News soon reached Uşak of the terrible events and Christophorus, accompanied by several men from The Anatolian Carpet Manufacturers Ltd. raced home. After the dead were buried, all the villagers pulled together to repair and rebuild some of the houses. It would take weeks and needed to be done before the onset of winter. In the meantime, they were housed in the schoolhouse, the han, the hamam, and several Greek homes. Marika Stavrides gave up her house again for Cemal, Saniye and Ayşe Baci. On hearing of the devastation, Ferit Ali sent out whatever furniture and mattresses he could muster together, along with a few sacks of grain and vegetables. By the time the cold blizzards swept across the Anatolian plateau, most of the houses were ready to be occupied once more. Surrounded by ghosts, the bleakness of winter only served to shroud the villages in a melancholic air.

CHAPTER 27

The Miracle

Aspasia was in the garden with Elpida, sorting out charcoal and twigs for the fire when Saniye appeared at the gate. Her face was beaming with happiness. As soon as Elpida saw who it was, she dropped her twigs and ran to her. Saniye scooped her up and kissed her cheeks.

'I've brought something back to you,' Saniye smiled, handing her a cloth-covered parcel.

Aspasia wiped her hands on her apron and took it. It was the silver icon.

'I'd forgotten all about it, what with the recent events.'

'Well I hadn't. It has been in a box near my bed ever since you gave it to me. Thankfully, it was the box that protected it from the damage wrought by the soldiers.'

Aspasia studied her friend's moon-shaped face with its dark almond eyes and curved eyebrows that almost joined at the bridge of her nose and burst out laughing. There was no doubt about it. Saniye had that unmistakable happy, healthy look.

'*Theo mou*, Saniye,' Aspasia smiled. 'Are you telling me it actually worked?'

'Sister, that is exactly what I am saying. It's a miracle. Your God has looked favourably on us. I am three months gone. I couldn't wait to tell you. I shall go to your church and light a candle. '

Aspasia kissed her friend's cheek and at the same took Elpida from her.

'You shouldn't be picking up heavy things now — even Elpida. You must take care.'

She ushered Saniye to the divan, plumped up the cushions to put behind her back, and then went to the glass cabinet.

'This is the best news I've heard in a long time. It calls for a celebration.'

She poured out two tiny glasses of a glowing, amber-coloured liqueur and gave one to Saniye who raised it to her nose. It smelt like an aromatic medicine.

'You know I don't drink alcohol,' she said.

Aspasia told her it was a special type of herbal liqueur called a digestif.

'The owner of the Hotel Europa gave it to Christophorus when he heard of our troubles. It was left by the Germans after the war. Apparently it contains many herbs that have calming and relaxing effects. God knows, I think we can all do with that after what we've been through.'

Saniye sipped it cautiously and then asked for another. Aspasia obliged, pouring herself another at the same time. Then put the bottle away.

'That's it until the child is born,' she said adamantly.

Elpida wanted to show Saniye her latest doll.

She took it from the child's hand and remarked on its

beauty. 'If I can have a little one like her, I will be the happiest woman in the world,' she said, feigning a spitting sound to ward of the evil eye.

Aspasia thought back to their last conversation when Saniye wished for a boy who would marry Elpida.

'I thought you wanted a boy?'

Saniye's smile disappeared. 'Women have a hard life, but men have it worse. This war has shown me that. I couldn't bear to lose a son in a war brought about by thoughtless politicians.'

Aspasia agreed. They talked more about the pregnancy and calculated that the child would be born sometime around July 1922. After the French clock chimed, this time making them smile once more, Saniye got up to leave. She promised to come by and resume her weaving and embroidery. Aspasia looked forward to it. She watched her friend jauntily walk down the hill to the meydan and crossed herself. For the moment, she had chosen to keep her own secret. It was possible she was pregnant herself. She would wait and see if her blood returned. To celebrate prematurely would be to invite the evil eye. In a world full of superstition, that was to be avoided at all costs.

*

One month later, Aspasia had still not menstruated and she began to suffer from morning sickness again. This time it was even more severe than when she was pregnant with Elpida. She kept her joy to herself until Christophorus knew. Needless to say, he was overjoyed.

'Oh my golden one,' he smiled, kissing her belly. 'God is really looking down on us. This calls for a celebration.'

195

He went straight back out and asked Tassos to buy him a sheep from one of the shepherds. It's too cold to celebrate outside, but if you throw open the Sun Coffee House for the women also, I will invite all the villagers to celebrate with us. The next day, the aroma of roast lamb filled the meydan. The women cooked vegetables, bread and dips, and brought them to the coffee house which had been laid out with tables around the walls and a small place for the musicians and dancing. Only two musicians turned up; the others had either been killed or had gone to join the Nationalists.

Cemal and Saniye were also there and much to Saniye's joy, everyone congratulated them on her pregnancy. The forthcoming birth of two more children in the village was a much needed tonic in times of desolation. Cemal, dressed in a spotless white şalvar over which he wore a colourful embroidered waistcoat made by Saniye, beamed with pride, and for once put all negative thoughts about the Greeks behind him. Life had dealt him a bitter blow but he had made the most of it. With the aid of crutches, he could move quite well. The marriage with Fatma was never raised again by anyone. Even Aspasia was not sure if he knew she died in childbirth.

As the evening drew to a close, everyone cheered the happy couples.

'You haven't told us when the child will be born?' Tassos said.

'At the end of August,' replied Christophorus.

CHAPTER 28

The House of Ill Luck

It was a Saturday evening and the Hotel Europa was filled to capacity. The orchestra started to play a Viennese Waltz.

'Would you care to dance, my love?' Christophorus said, offering his hand to Aspasia.

She smiled. 'I'd be delighted.'

With the palm of his hand on the small of her back, he ushered her on to the dance floor and took her in his arms.

'I am blissfully happy,' she whispered in his ear as they swirled around the room. 'It's hard to imagine that there were times when I never thought I would smile again.'

'You look so beautiful tonight,' Christophorus replied. 'Pregnancy suits you.'

Her dark, silken hair and gold earrings glinted under the soft lights of the Hotel Europa's dining room chandeliers, and the soft skin of her neck and breasts, swollen from her pregnancy, reminded him of the skin of a glistening ripe apricot in the morning dew. Aspasia had always been beautiful, but in Christophorus's eyes, womanhood had made her a goddess.

They danced through a few more waltzes, and then sat down again to peruse the menu.

'What will you have for dessert?' Christophorus asked. 'I can highly recommend the French Crème brûlée, the crêpes, and the pistachio sorbet.'

'Not altogether,' Aspasia smiled. She picked up her fan and began fanning herself.

'I will have the strawberries,' she said, patting her round belly. 'I am afraid anything heavier may not agree with the child.'

Christophorus ordered. Deliciously ripe strawberries arrived in a crystal bowl served on a small silver plate. Christophorus ordered flambéed crêpes which were prepared at the table.

'No wonder you have put on weight,' Aspasia teased. 'If you eat like this every night, then you are thoroughly spoilt. How can you bear my simple koftes and dolmades after such wonderful food?'

Christophorus laughed. 'Your food is made with love, my darling. Nothing beats that.'

The conversation turned to her pregnancy. Aspasia was now seven months gone and already the child kicked intermittently in her belly. Yet, she was still worried. Over the past few months, the bouts of sickness disappeared, but then came back for days on end, leaving her with a lack of energy. It was the reason she was spending a few days in Uşak. Christophorus had arranged for her to see a Greek doctor.

'I think the pills the doctor gave me are working,' she said. 'At least I feel a lot better.'

Christophorus reached across the table and held her hand. 'I know he thinks there is nothing wrong, all the same, it might be a good idea for you to stay here when the time comes. Just in case of complications.'

Aspasia smiled. 'You fuss too much, my beloved. He has assured me that I will be fine if I take the pills. There's nothing more to be said. Besides, Saniye is about to give birth and she needs me.'

'You are obstinate,' Christophorus replied, 'but it's one of the things I love about you.'

*

Marika Stavrides was in the garden playing with Elpida when Aspasia arrived home.

'What's all this?' she asked, watching one of Ancient Yusuf's boys carry a wooden crib though the gate along with several other parcels.

'It's a crib for the little one. Elpida never had one.'

Elpida put one of her dolls in it and started to rock it. 'Is that for my new brother, mama?'

'It is *matakia mou,*' Aspasia replied, laughing at the way Elpida was convinced she would have a brother.

Her mother-in-law shook her head. 'My son spoils you,' she said. 'What else did you buy?'

A few more silks and embroidery threads. I need to add to my children's dowry.'

They both laughed.

'Tell me, Mama, how is Saniye?'

'I saw her yesterday. She wasn't feeling too well. The time is getting close and Ayşe Baci has stopped tending the goats to be by her side. I pray all goes well this time.'

Aspasia decided to pay Saniye a visit. On the way, she noticed Greek troops heading towards the meydan. A few villagers stood and stared, praying they would not stay. Saniye was resting on a mattress under the mulberry tree when Aspasia arrived. Ayşe Baci was coaxing her to eat a little yoghurt mixed with chopped dates, cinnamon and liquorice. She appeared lifeless and her round face looked drawn and she had dark shadows around her eyes.

'What ails you, dear friend?' Aspasia asked.

Saniye could barely speak. Aspasia felt her forehead. She had a fever and was sweating. The look in her eyes conveyed something was drastically wrong.

Ayşe Baci pulled her aside.

'I am fearful for her. I've seen this many times before. The child hasn't moved for a while now. Either she or the child will die.'

Aspasia did not want to hear such negativity, yet she knew things were bad. She called for her mother-in-law to take a look at Saniye for herself.

'We must do something to induce the pregnancy?' Marika Stavrides asked. 'Time is running out.'

Ayşe Baci agreed.' I've given her tisanes of cotton-root and thyme, and I've been feeding her dates and liquorice.'

Saniye clutched her belly and cried out. Marika suggested they bring her inside and check her cervix. After making her comfortable on the divan, the women pulled away her pantaloons and examined her.

'The cervix is ripening,' Ayşe Baci said. 'But I don't like the look of this.'

A small trickle of blood was starting to flow. The women

decided to force her to stand and walk around the room. Saniye screamed in agony when they tried to move her. A few hours later, her waters broke.

'It's going to be a long night,' Marika said, with a heavy sigh.

Afraid that the situation was not good for Aspasia's own pregnancy, Marika told her to go home.

'Elpida needs you. There's nothing you can do here. What will be, will be. I will let you know if there is any news.'

Aspasia left the house with a heavy heart. She feared for her own unborn child and crossed herself. *Stay safe little one.*

As the first rays of light slid through the slatted shutters, Aspasia awoke to find her mother-in-law standing at the foot of the bed. Aspasia threw back the coverlet.

'In the name of the Virgin, what has happened?'

'The child was stillborn,' she replied. 'It was a girl.'

'And Saniye?'

Marika crossed herself. 'Give praise to the Virgin, she will live, although she is weak.'

Aspasia threw on some clothes and hurried to Pınarbaşı. Several women had already gathered at the house, keening like cats. Ayşe Baci stood outside the door and wailed.

'This house is cursed,' she screamed at the top of her voice. 'It is the house of ill luck. Allah forgive our sins.'

Cemal sat in the garden staring at the chickens and smoking his narghile. He cursed anyone who went near him. Saniye slept, despite the commotion going on around her. Aspasia sat next to her and stroked her face wondering if she would ever get over this.

CHAPTER 29

The River of Tears

The Greek army was on the move again and the villagers took to sitting in the meydan for hours on end just to pick up snippets of news. They soon discovered that due to the failure of peace negotiations in Paris, the Greek army had decided not to evacuate Asia Minor, but to stay on and re-deploy troops to the areas already under their control. Now the soldiers were heading eastwards again to join those still entrenched in the uplands of Anatolia. The Greeks of Stavrodromi prayed for them. The Turks of Pınarbaşı remained silent, keeping their thoughts to themselves. It was a tense time.

Throughout the first half of August, Saniye was so depressed she refused to leave the house. Cemal took to the plateau and stayed there for nights on end, whilst Ayşe Baci, tired and broken, was left to pick up the pieces. After making sure the last bales of carpets had left for Smyrna, Ferit Ali gave Christophorus time off to be with his wife until the child was born. He was looking forward to it.

The first news that something had gone wrong was at the

end of August when Damocles and Tassos knocked on his door in the early hours of the morning.

'The news is not good, Christophorus, the Turks have won a decisive battle against our troops. The Greeks put up fierce resistance, but the Nationalists broke through their lines. I am afraid the Greeks left it too late. They waited too long.'

Christophorus felt his legs give way.

'We have to leave,' said Tassos. 'Now, before it's too late.'

'And go where? It's preposterous.'

Damocles told him to get dressed and accompany them to the meydan where the men were already gathering to discuss the situation. He kissed his sleeping wife on the forehead and left the house. It was still dark and the Greeks gathered by lantern light around the fountain. There was no sign of the Turks. Father Andronikos was the first to speak.

'My children, this is a catastrophe. The retreating soldiers are known to be heading this way and will be here soon. After the last time, we need to be prepared.'

'What do you want us to do, Father?' someone asked.

'The soldiers will spare our neighbours no mercy. We must warn them. Even our own village is not safe. The Greek army has a scorched earth policy. Everything is to be destroyed.'

This news was simply too overwhelming for most of them to comprehend, but after seeing what the soldiers had done almost a year ago, they were well aware of the implications. They listened stoically, but in the pit of their stomachs, they felt fear.

'We must leave. That is what I am saying. Get your women and children and flee. Head for Uşak. You will be safe there. Now go,' he said, shooing them away, 'before it's too late.'

The villagers ran back to their homes, whilst Father

Andronikos went to the house of his friend, Imam Süleyman, and advised him to warn his people.

Christophorus called at his mother's house first and told her to prepare to move out straight away. When she protested, he grew angry telling her there would be time for questions later. Right now, she was to obey him.

'Prepare a bag and wait with Tassos in the meydan. Do as he says,' Christophorus shouted, slamming the door behind him.

Aspasia had just woken and was wondering what was going on.

'Where have you been?' she said, rubbing her aching back.

When Christophorus told her, the blood drained from her face.

'I can't go, Christophorus. I'll never make it. The pains are getting shorter and stronger.'

Christophorus paced the room, banging his fist on the side of his temple. 'Why now?' he shouted, more to himself than Aspasia. 'Why now?'

He told her to pack a bag but she pleaded with him not to make her leave.

'Take Elpida and go,' she cried. 'As for me, it's impossible. That ride will be the death of me. You know I am not as strong as I was when Elpida was born.'

Elpida was not used to her parents arguing in this way, and she started to cry. Christophorus was in no mood for tears. He told Aspasia to dress her while he packed a bag for her. When this was done, he picked up Elpida and held her tightly with one arm and the bag in the other.

'Kiss your child goodbye,' he said. 'She is going with my mother.'

A distraught Aspasia cupped Elpida's little face and smothered her with kisses.

'Go with grandmother, my precious one. I will see you soon.'

Christophorus carried Elpida to the meydan where the oxcarts were quickly filling with villagers, their baggage, and an assortment of other household goods. He deposited her on his mother's lap.

'Go straight to Ferit Ali,' he ordered. 'He will look after you both.'

He kissed Elpida and then his mother's tear-streaked cheeks and ran back to the house ignoring both his daughter's cries and his mother's. When he arrived home, Aspasia lay on the floor with severe pains. Without the women, Christophorus had no idea what to do. Then he heard a knock on the door. It was Saniye. Christophorus was too emotional to speak. Saniye should have left. Why was she here now?

'I will not forsake my sister,' she said. 'Allah would slam the gates of Paradise in my face.'

She took one look at Aspasia and realized the child would come at any moment. Thankfully, her waters hadn't broken as yet.

'Christophorus, we have to get you both away from here. Father Andronikos warned us, but I am warning you. It's too dangerous to stay. I know a safe place where she can give birth. It's not far away, but we must go now.'

For once in his life, Christophorus stopped giving orders and followed Saniye's instructions. He went to the han and saddled his horse along with a donkey that stood nearby. Ancient Yusuf and his boys were nowhere in sight. All the oxcarts had gone, leaving behind several piles of assorted furniture and mattresses that could not be carried. The meydan was eerily empty and the clip-clopping of the animals on the cobblestones broke the silence like church bells at Easter.

Christophorus helped Aspasia onto his horse whilst Saniye filled a woven saddle bag full of their belongings and tied it securely on the mule. Rather than take one of the main exits, she led them out of the village via a narrow path that meandered past the Turkish communal oven and up towards the plateau where the Turks kept their wheat fields and a threshing circle. When they reached the top, Christophorus looked down on the deserted villages below. He felt a lump rise in his throat, wondering if he would ever return.

Years spent tending goats with Cemal and her mother-in-law had equipped Saniye with a profound knowledge of the plateau. She knew it like the back of her hand. They rode in silence in the heat of the day for several hours, stopping only to give Aspasia a sip of water. Ahead of them the ground shimmered in a heat haze. Further afield, plumes of smoke curled into a cloudless blue sky. The retreating Greek troops were burning villages.

Soon the plateau reached a point where it appeared to drop off the earth. Below was a vast, steep canyon that stretched as far as the eye could see. Christophorus pinched himself to make sure he wasn't dreaming. He had grown up in the area but had never known this place existed. The rocky terrain of the plateau burst into a dramatic sea of variegated greens. Large swathes of pines, oaks and cedar, merged into rocky outcrops of rockrose, broom, milk vetch, and wild marjoram. A thin band of a river glistened like a mirror in the bright sunlight.

Christophorus exchanged glances with Saniye.

'Don't worry,' she said. 'I've been here many times with the goats. It's steep, but it's not as dangerous as it looks.'

Saniye led them slowly down a goat track that meandered between the rocks and scrub. The animals were sure-footed, but Aspasia's pain was worsening. Saniye feared her waters would break at any moment, leaving them exposed.

'Just a little further, Sister,' she said to Aspasia, 'and then we will rest.'

The winding path took them along a narrow ledge which led to several caves in the cliff face. Saniye tied her donkey to a tree and helped Christophorus with Aspasia.

'No-one will find us here. It can't be seen from the top of the canyon.'

The pair had no sooner got Aspasia into a cave when her waters broke. *May the Virgin protect her*, Christophorus mumbled to himself. Saniye quickly untied the baggage and laid a cloth on the floor for Aspasia to lie on. She dribbled a little water onto a small sponge and handed it to him.

'She has a fever. Keep her head cool with this while I fetch some wood and make a fire.'

Christophorus followed Saniye's instructions whilst she disappeared in search of firewood. For the first time in his life, he felt vulnerable and lost. After a while, Saniye finally returned with a stack of firewood strapped to her back.

'How is she?' she asked.

'Not good. She's becoming delirious.'

'Keep bathing her. It's important,' Saniye replied.

They had a small fire going which illuminated the cave with dancing shadows. Saniye took the sponge from him and continued wiping Aspasia's face and brow.

'All we can do is to wait and pray. It won't be long, and at least she is safe here.'

By sunset, Aspasia's pains worsened and she was writhing in pain. One minute she was lucid, the next, she hardly recognized them. In one of her clearer moments, she clasped Christophorus's hand.

'My darling, I fear that this time I may not make it. You must be prepared for the worst, but always remember that not even death will part us.'

Christophorus begged her not to talk like this.

She reached out and gently touched his lips. 'Shush!' she whispered, gasping for breath. 'I want you to listen to me. A child that cries will give you away. For the sake of the others, think carefully...'

Another spasm of pain caused her to stop mid-sentence. Confused and distressed, Christophorus stepped outside for a while to clear his mind. The sun was beginning to sink behind the escarpment, drenching the canyon in molten streaks of reds and violet. The fiery colours were replaced by inky blue-black shadows that descended over the cliff face like a shroud, until the canyon was plunged into darkness.

'Come inside,' Saniye shouted. 'It's not safe out there. You could slip.'

The night passed slowly, and still Aspasia did not give birth. Saniye now feared that both mother and child would lose their life. She was at her wits end. At the first light of day, they heard the sound of hooves approaching the cave. It was Ayşe Baci on Cemal's donkey. Christophorus was frantic to find out what was happening back in the village, but Ayşe Baci refused to talk about it saying that it was Aspasia they should think about now.

One look at the poor woman and she knew the situation was dire. Aspasia was fading in and out of consciousness. Saniye took her mother aside to discuss what to do.

'We must bring this baby into the world ourselves. There's no time to spare,' Ayşe Baci told her.

They asked Christophorus to leave for a while. Reluctantly, he did as asked. Ayşe Baci forced Aspasia to drink a cup full of her medicine and the women then prepared her for the birth. Outside the cave, Christophorus sat on a rock and put his hands over his ears to block out Aspasia's screams that echoed through the canyon. Then there was silence. He took his hands away from his ears and listened. The silence was worse than the screams. Then came the unmistakable cry of a newborn. He jumped up and raced back to the cave. *It's over*, he said to himself. *It's finally over.*

When he entered the cave, his happiness quickly faded. The look on Saniye and Ayşe Baci's faces told him it had not gone well. The ordeal had been too much for her. Aspasia was dead. Grief-stricken, he fell on his knees and cradled her lifeless body in his arms.

'There was nothing we could do,' lamented Ayşe Baci. 'But we did save the child. You have another girl.'

Saniye sat by the fire, cradling the newborn. Tears blinded her eyes, but she took solace in the fact that they had at least saved her friend's child.

After some hours, Ayşe Baci began to tell them what took place in the village. The Greek army arrived a few hours after they left. Worn out, dejected, and humiliated, their anger was even worse than the last time. Cemal and Ayşe Baci watched it all from their hideout overlooking the village. Pınarbaşı was razed to the ground. Then they started on Stavrodromi, looting and setting fire to several buildings until their commander urged them on. Worst of all, they found some of the Turkish villagers hiding — two old men and a woman who could barely walk. With them was Ancient Yusuf. They hanged them all from the plane trees in the meydan. A few hours later, the Nationalists arrived. What the Greek soldiers left untouched, the Turkish soldiers finished off. Hardly anything of both villages remained.

'We are all finished,' lamented Ayşe Baci, slapping her chest to ease the heartache.

Christophorus could barely take it all in. It was more than he could comprehend. After some time deep in sorrow and thought, he decided he had to get to Uşak at all costs. It was the only way to save himself. More importantly, his mother and Elpida would be anxiously waiting for him. If he didn't reach them soon, he feared for their safety. He looked at Aspasia lying in such an inhospitable place.

'We must bury her first,' he said, touching her cold lips with his fingertips. 'We can't leave her here.'

'We'll take her back to the village and give her a proper burial,' Ayşe Baci replied. 'It should be safe to return now.'

She went outside and made several whistling sounds. In the distance, the same calls were repeated.

'It's Cemal. He's given us the all clear.'

In the midst of a river of tears, Saniye managed a smile. After all the heartache, Cemal had finally come through for her. The war had made him despise the Greeks, but he didn't despise Aspasia and Christophorus. For Saniye and his mother's sake, he would help them escape.

Ayşe Baci reached into her bag and handed Christophorus some clothes.

'Put them on,' she said. 'They're Cemal's.'

He took off his clothes and replaced them with Cemal's baggy, white *şalvar*, a dark shirt and a waistcoat with raised coils of embroidery, and a striped cotton cummerbund, tied at the side and hanging below the knee. Cemal was a small man but thankfully the clothes were so baggy they fitted. Finally, he placed the red fez firmly on his head. Could he pass for a Turk, he asked the two women? Their reply was that he had no choice.

They wrapped Aspasia's body in the cloth she had lain on and placed it on Christophorus's horse. He rode with her whilst Saniye carried the child. When they reached the top of the escarpment Cemal was waiting for them. After determining it was safe to continue, they headed back to the village.

The sight of both villages broke his heart. The once vibrant hamlets were nothing more than burnt-out ruins. Smoke hung in the air, Turkish flags decorated the trees, and few buildings were still left standing. Several heavily armed Turks were sitting idly in a circle in the meydan sorting through a pile of belongings. Thankfully, the bodies had been removed from the trees. When the men saw them, they fired a volley of shots in the air and came over.

'Halt. What are you doing here?' one of them asked.

Having grown up here, Christophorus was fluent in Turkish, but Saniye advised him to say as little as possible. 'If they suspect you're Greek, they'll tear you to pieces,' she warned.

'We live here.' Cemal replied. He pointed to Pınarbaşı. 'My house is in ruins. Thanks be to Allah, we have survived, but our sister has died in childbirth and we must bury her.'

After checking that they were not carrying weapons, the man stepped forward to inspect the body. When he saw Aspasia's dark hair, he was satisfied.

'Be on your way, Brother,' he replied. 'May she be granted peace in the garden of Paradise.'

It was decided to bury Aspasia in the Islamic cemetery to avoid unwelcomed attention. Christophorus lowered Aspasia's body into the earth, said a prayer and tearfully walked away, leaving Saniye and Ayşe Baci to cover her with soil. They placed a stone on the grave and headed back to the village.

'This is where we go our separate ways,' said Cemal. 'Tell the men you want to go to Uşak and fight with the Nationalists and they will leave you alone.'

Christophorus was filled with so much grief he could barely speak. 'If I live to be a hundred, I will never be able to thank you enough.'

'No words are necessary, Brother,' Cemal replied. He scooped up a dusty piece of earth, let the soil slip through his fingers into a handkerchief, secured it with a knot and gave it to Christophorus. 'Our hearts and our lives are intertwined. We are the seeds of this good earth. Now it is time to scatter those seeds.'

After saying their final goodbyes, Christophorus stepped forward to take the baby from Saniye.

'She is yours, Christophorus, but think hard. This land has changed. Uşak may not be your final resting place. Are you able to look after one so young? She needs her mother's milk. I still have milk after I lost my child. I can feed and nourish her. Let her stay here. I will be her milk mother. I will love her and care for her as my own.'

Christophorus's heart pounded in his chest. He knew the

importance of a milk mother in Turkish life. She would always be a respected member of the family, but to leave his daughter behind, that was something else.'

Saniye held out the child for him to take. 'A child that cries will give you away,' she said. 'For the sake of the others, think carefully. You have Elpida to think about now.'

Christophorus felt a lump rise in his throat. They were the same words Aspasia uttered before she died. *What did she mean? What if he must escape to Smyrna or Constantinople: Greece even? Would his daughter survive? Were they warning him of imminent danger?* Christophorus's mind was a whirlpool of thoughts.

Saniye could see the heartache in his eyes. She placed the child on the ground and started to walk away.

'Wait,' Christophorus called out. He picked up his daughter, gave her a kiss, and put her in Saniye's arms. 'You are right. Where I am going, I cannot look after her. I believe this is what Aspasia would have wanted: a token of your deep friendship. Look after her well.'

He mounted his horse and headed towards the Turkish guards. Saniye, Cemal and Ayşe Baci watched to make sure things went smoothly. The guards waved him on. Christophorus resisted the urge to look back. His heart had shattered into a thousand pieces, but he must now concentrate on survival.

CHAPTER 30

The Escape

Nea Ionia, Athens 1970

Christos turned off the tape recorder and sat back in his chair with his head bent, silent and thoughtful. His mother sobbed quietly into her handkerchief whilst the man at the centre of the story, his grandfather, still had his eyes closed as if opening them would break the spell and snap him out of the old world into the present.

'I had no idea,' Elpida said, 'No idea at all. And to think I don't recall any of this.'

She shook her head, trying to take it all in. Christophorus opened his eyes.

'You were only four years old. It is to be expected,' he replied. 'After we came to Greece, I thought it better not to talk about it. Perhaps I was wrong. Who knows? What is done, is done.'

During the course of his life, Christos had heard many refugee stories but none touched him as much as this. He didn't blame his grandfather for his silence. Perhaps he would have done the same.

Elpida started to clear the table in readiness for the dessert and Christos offered to help. When they were alone in the kitchen, she burst into tears again.

Christos put a comforting arm around her. 'It's okay, Mama, *Papou's* story has shaken us both.'

They observed Christophorus through the kitchen window. His hand reached towards a loquat bloom and a smile crossed his face.

'Look at him,' Elpida said. 'He's thinking of mama.'

Christos agreed. 'He doesn't seem to look so sad any more. I think getting this story off his chest has done him the world of good.'

'How did we escape?' Elpida asked, pouring out three small cups of coffee. 'I don't remember that.'

'Come on. Let me carry this tray outside for you and we'll find out.'

Elpida cut a slice of bougatsa and gave them all a piece.

'How are you feeling, Papa?' she asked. 'Has all this been too much for you?'

'Not at all. In fact, I feel as though a great weight has been lifted off my chest.'

'I don't remember how we escaped,' she said, throwing a quick glance towards her son. 'Can you remind me?'

'Certainly.'

Christos changed the tape and switched the recorder on again.

'We're ready when you are, *Papou*.'

*

Uşak, September 1922

When Christophorus reached Uşak, he got the shock of his life. Much of the town lay in ruins. The retreating Greeks had even tried to burn down the apple orchards. Turkish soldiers were everywhere, just as they had been at the outbreak of war in 1914, only this time there were hardly any Greeks. They had either fled, been captured, or killed. Uppermost in his mind was to find Ferit Ali's house in the well-off neighbourhood where the rich Greeks, Armenians and Levantines had lived.

Ferit Ali's home was a stone building, hidden from the road by a large garden. The entrance was through a wrought iron gate which hung precariously from a single hinge as though it had been hit by a heavy vehicle. Christophorus made his way along the driveway to the house, but his heart sank when he saw the sight of the beautiful garden lying in ruins. The once perfumed rose bushes lay twisted and tangled amidst the oleander and assortment of debris. Two large guard dogs appeared from the side of the house, bounding towards him baying for blood. He froze. At that moment the front door opened and he heard a shrill whistle. The dogs stopped only seconds before attacking him.

'What do you want?' a voice called out.

It was Ferit Ali.

When he heard his familiar voice, Christophorus wanted to shout out with joy.

'It is I, Efendim. Christophorus.'

Ferit Ali had to look twice. 'I never thought you'd make it,' he smiled, slapping him on the back whilst ushering him into the house. 'And these clothes; I thought you were a Turk.' He paused. 'Where's Aspasia?'

Christophorus couldn't bring himself to say she was dead, but Ferit Ali could tell by the look on his face that something terrible had happened.

'Elpida and my mother,' Christophorus asked. 'Are they here? Are they safe?'

'They are quite safe. I tried to persuade them to leave with the other Greeks heading for Smyrna, but they refused to go without you.'

He took them into the sitting room where his wife and sister were preparing afternoon tea for their two guests.

'Prepare another plate,' Ferit Ali said to his wife. 'We have a special guest.'

At the sight of Christophorus, dressed as a Turk, his mother let out a sharp cry; at first in fear, then followed by happiness. Elpida saw through the clothing.

'Papa, Papa' she shouted, running into his arms.

The joy at seeing them both again was more than he could bear. He hugged his daughter so hard she cried out in pain. His mother clasped both his hands and brought them to her lips.

'My precious son, God has looked after you.' Her eyes looked towards the door, in anticipation. 'Aspasia,' she whispered. 'Where is she?'

Christophorus tried to fight back the tears. 'She wasn't strong enough this time. She didn't make it.'

Elpida was too young to take it in, but his words were too much for his mother. Ferit Ali's wife tried her best to comfort her. It was to no avail. Marika Stavrides had loved Aspasia like her own daughter and her heart was broken.

'The child?' she asked, tears streaking her face. 'What happened, my son? Please tell me.'

Christophorus couldn't bear the thought of telling them the truth.

'It was stillborn,' he lied.

Almost immediately, discussions centred on what to do next. There was no doubt that things had gone badly for the Greeks. With Uşak now in the hands of the Turks, and the carpet factories decimated, Christophorus knew that if he stayed, he would either be killed or marched away to a labour battalion. Uppermost in his mind was his daughter and mother. When he thought things could not get any worse, the news came through that Smyrna was on fire. Ferit Ali decided that the best course of action was for them to try and reach Constantinople, and it was imperative they leave immediately. He hatched a plan for them to dress as Turks and accompany him, together with a consignment of carpets to be delivered to a warehouse there. All the carpets in the factory had either been stolen or destroyed, but he did have some stock-piled at home. Now was the time to get rid of them. They would have to go by oxcart, and the journey was expected to take several weeks due to unrest. There were no other options as the rail lines had either been blown up or were in the hands of the Nationalists. He would arrange the paperwork for them straight away.

After a few days, the carpets were loaded on to the cart and the four set out for Constantinople. Marika's documents stated she was Ferit Ali's mother, and Elpida, who was told not to speak Greek when anyone was around, was his grand-daughter. As for Christophorus, he was a Turkish buyer with premises in Sultanahmet. It was an audacious plan, but it worked. Ferit Ali accompanied them into the heart of Constantinople, and made sure they had had somewhere safe to stay. The pair shook hands for the last time, and Ferit Ali returned to Uşak.

Having reached the safety of Constantinople, Christophorus, together with his mother and daughter, disposed of their Turkish papers and managed to get new ones from the Allied authorities still governing the city. The documents stated that they were Greek Orthodox residents of Anatolia and now officially homeless. A month later, they boarded a ship bound for Piraeus.

CHAPTER 31

The Ghost Village

Nea Ionia, Athens 1970

For a while, the conversation centred on the kindness of Ferit Ali and the huge personal debt Christophorus owed him for saving them. He had risked not only his own life, but that of his family's as well.

'And you never contacted each other again?' Christos asked, 'Even after the population exchange?'

'No,' Christophorus replied, sharply.

Elpida and Christos exchanged glances. There was something in the dismissive way he answered that made them think he was not telling the truth.

Christos looked at his watch. It was almost midnight yet he wasn't tired. The story had fired his imagination, and he couldn't wait to get back to the university and pull it all together. Despite the revelations, there was one thing that preyed on both of their minds, and no-one wanted to mention it. In the end it was left to Elpida.

'Papa, you said I had a sister. Do you know what happened to her?'

Christophorus stared at the loquat blooms. Suddenly the words had dried up.

Elpida wouldn't let up. 'I cannot believe that you wouldn't want to know — your own flesh and blood. Tell me Papa; tell me what happened to her? I will not sleep in peace until I know.'

Christophorus sighed heavily. He knew he had to finish what he'd begun.

'Go to my room and bring me the photograph,' he replied.

Elpida did as he asked. When she picked it up, several shards of glass fell away.

'I will replace it tomorrow,' she said, handing it to him.

Christophorus picked up a knife and twisted the small latch at the back. In doing so, the rest of the glass fell out and the frame fell apart. Elpida and Christos got the shock of their lives. Behind the photograph lay a faded white envelope. In it, was a photograph and a letter. Christophorus told her it was sent to the Refugee Commission Offices in Piraeus. He cleared his throat and started to read.

Uşak 1936

For Christophorus Stavrides Efendi, son of Stavrodromi, I write this letter in the hope that you are alive and in good health. For some time now, my mind has been preoccupied with thoughts about contacting you. In light of recent events, that time has come.

The day you walked out of our lives, you left us the most precious gift a human being could ever give — your daughter. We named her Leyla and she became the light of our life. *Every time we looked into her beautiful eyes, we saw her mother; when we heard her laughter, it was her mother's. When we saw her kind and caring ways, they were her mother's. If she had been created in my daughter-in-law's own womb, she could not have been loved more.*

After we parted ways, we lived in another village for a few months, but with little food and the countryside in ruins, our life became a misery and we moved to Uşak in the hope that a bigger town would provide us with a livelihood. For a while, the carpet factories lay idle. The Christian weavers had all left, and there were few skilled enough to take their place. Saniye suggested we contact Ferit Ali Efendi. When she told him who she was, he took us all in and looked after us. It was due to his kind heart that we were soon given a home again.

Like most of us, the wretched war had broken Ferit Ali Efendi's spirit, and not even his wife could coax him out of his melancholy. The following spring, when the snows melted and the blossoms lightened the soul, Saniye told him she wanted to make carpets like those she had made with Aspasia. He remembered them with fondness and agreed to set her up with a loom in the factory. Before long, she was joined by others who admired her skill. After this, our life began to improve once more and the darkness of war was replaced with hope.

When Leyla was still a young child, she displayed a natural aptitude for weaving and would sit by Saniye's side watching and copying her actions. They were wonderful, precious moments and filled our hearts with joy. By the time, she reached her twelfth birthday; we decided to make a visit back to our village. Some of the Anatolian villages had been rebuilt and were beginning to prosper under the new Republic. Schools were being built, and trade, railways and transport improved. It breaks my heart to tell you that our own village was not one of them. It lies deserted and in ruins, much as it did when we last saw it. The only thing that remains intact is the Fountain of the Sun and Moon where we set out a cloth on the stone seat and ate our food.

Before returning back to Uşak, Saniye took Leyla for a walk. When they reached your house, parts of the walls were still standing. The roof had caved in, the windows no longer had shutters or glass, and the garden was completely over-grown, but the fruit trees still bore fruit: a small sign of life to remind us of happier times. Where once our ears were filled with the idle chatter of women, the laughter of children, and the music of celebrations in the meydan, now the only sound is that of the wind whistling through the broken windows. The village belongs to the past.

All this brings me to the part that I have deliberated over telling you. It was not long after this visit that our lives changed again. Saniye and Leyla were returning from the factory when they were struck down by a runaway horse and cart. In that moment, they were lost to us forever. Cemal has turned into a recluse. Not a day goes by when he doesn't sit cross-legged on the floor, reciting the Koran and twisting his prayer beads. Ill luck had been our companion for many years — until Leyla. I am enclosing a photograph of her. It is the only one we have but it belongs to you. It would be Saniye's wish that it sits alongside that of Aspasia and Elpida.

As for myself, I am nearing the end, and my eyes no longer see the light. I am dictating this letter to the wife of Ferit Ali

Efendi, as our friend, praise be to Almighty Allah, passed through the gates of Paradise during the winter. She is taking it to someone who writes Greek and is assured of keeping our secret. Let it be known that you were always in our hearts.

May Allah keep you safe,

Your friend,

Ayşe Baci

Christophorus looked at the photograph. The emotions that he had bottled up for so long burst forth, and the tears fell freely when he looked at the young girl sitting by the loom. She was knotting a carpet and at the same time facing the camera. Her bright smile and laughing eyes were infectious.

'She is the image of her mother,' he said, touching her face with the tips of his fingers.

He handed it to Elpida who brought it to her lips and kissed it. Sadness mixed with happiness. All she could think of was that she had a sister; someone who had been raised with as much love as she had. It tore her heart apart, yet she felt a sense of elation at discovering her. The photograph united them all.

'Why didn't you want to tell me this earlier, Papa?' Elpida asked.

I had to forget. I couldn't go on otherwise. Can you ever forgive me?'

Elpida put her arms around her father's frail shoulders. 'The truth hurts, but Ayşe Baci was right, Leyla is finally back where she belongs.'

Christos stood the photograph next to the one from the frame.

'There's one more thing that arrived with the letter.'

This time he went to his room himself. When he returned, he was carrying a small silk bag. Elpida looked astonished. She was the one who cleaned his room yet she had never seen it before.

He handed it to her as he sat back down.

'Open it,' he said.

Elpida's hands shook as she untied the cord and peaked inside.

'*Theo mou*, Papa,' she said, a lump rising in her throat. 'It's the silk slippers!'

She slid them out of the bag and held them in her hands, admiring their beauty and feeling their softness. Overcome with emotion, she closed her eyes and brought them to her nose, desperately trying to breathe in her mother's scent. After all the years, the childhood memories flooded back. She was too young to recall it all, but now the window to the past had opened again. Whether it was her imagination, she wasn't sure, but in her mind, she felt her mother's last embrace, cupping her face and kissing her.

'Thank you, Papa,' she said after a while. 'Thank you for opening your heart and sharing all this. Our past is something to be treasured. By unlocking it, you have given us something to be proud of.'

Christophorus told her he wanted her to have the slippers. 'I am sure your mother would have given you them herself were she still alive. Until now, I couldn't bear to part with them so I hid them in a tin. Another selfish act, I suppose.' He looked at his watch. 'And now, if you will excuse me, I feel sleepy. It's been a long day.'

Turning to Christos, he told him not to lose the tape as he was looking forward to seeing the documentary.

'I will do you Justice, *Papou*. You will be very proud, just you wait and see.'

Christophorus patted his grandson's shoulder affectionately and retired to his room. After undressing and carefully folding his clothes away, he combed his hair and moustache, and lay down on the bed. In that moment, Aspasia appeared.

'You did well, my precious,' she said in her honeyed voice.

Christophorus stared at her image until it faded. Then he pulled the cover over him and closed his eyes. A gentle breeze drifted through the open window, bringing with it the perfume of the loquat blossoms. His burden lifted, he slept like a baby for the first time in years.

Postscript

The seeds of *The Embroiderer, Seraphina's Song* and *The Carpet Weaver of Uşak* were sown during my years working as a carpet designer in Greece, 1972-78. The company was situated in a suburb of Athens populated by refugees from The Asia Minor Catastrophe, 1919-22. Working amongst these people, many of the older generation of whom still conversed in Turkish, I grew to understand the impact of the disaster and the intense yearning these people still held for Turkey, the land of their forefathers and a land in which they are still unable to reside. Significantly they shared a separate sense of identity, so much so that fifty years after the Catastrophe, many of them still referred to themselves as Mikrasiates (Asia Minor people) and still chose to intermarry.

The Asia Minor Catastrophe was a pivotal turning point in Greek/ Turkish relations which began a century earlier with the Greek War of Independence. The Ottoman Empire was at a turning point and for both Greeks and Turks, ultimately resulted in a war of attrition on both sides. Millions lost their lives and out of the ashes emerged two new nations – the Turkish Republic under the soldier statesman, Ataturk, and the Hellenic Republic – modern Greece.

Today, most of the white-washed prefabricated homes in the refugee neighbourhoods in Athens have been replaced by apartment blocks, but the street names still bear testament to their origins: Byzantium Street, Pergamum St, Anatolia St, Bouboulina St, and Misolonghi St. to name just a few. Whilst women no longer sit in their doorways on rush-bottomed chairs chatting to their neighbours and embroidering cloth for their daughter's dowry, and basement shops selling bric-a-brac and musical instruments from the 'old world' are few and far between, if we look closer, the history and the spirit of these people still resonates in their everyday lives; in their music, their food, the plethora of Turkish words and phrases that punctuate the Greek language, and the ancient belief in the evil eye. Most important of all, it is through the time-honoured tradition of storytelling that their memories are kept alive.

Although I designed oriental patterns for machine-made carpets, I also purchased an upright, Turkish-style carpet loom for my home, from a Greek lady whose first language was Turkish. The loom was exactly the same as the one Aspasia and Elpida would have woven on. The family also gave me their carpet beater and shears, which they would have brought with them from Turkey. Through watching these weavers, I gradually learnt the time-honoured tradition of hand-knotted carpets and dying. I still have some of those carpets in my home in Melbourne today.

*

The Carpet Weaver of Uşak is the third book in the Asia Minor trilogy. Each novel deals with a different aspect of the Asia Minor conflict and its effect on the lives of all involved.

The first novel, *The Embroiderer,* is epic in scale, and was written to portray the events that took place in the decades leading up to the catastrophe, and the aftermath, up until the German occupation of Greece 1941-44

In the second novel, *Seraphina's Song,* we glimpse the world that the majority of Asia Minor refugees lived in during the first decade following the great fire of Smyrna in 1922 and the population exchange of 1923. The conditions in the refugee settlements in and around Piraeus and other parts of Greece were appalling. Poverty and all that it brings – disease and despair, affected thousands. Music was one of the few ways the refugees could express their sorrows and hopes.

In *The Carpet Weaver of Uşak,* I wanted to portray the lives of the ordinary villagers throughout Anatolia. For most of these rural villages and hamlets, village life passed by in much the same way from one generation to another as it had for centuries. Whilst there were differences in ethnic groups and religions, for the most part, the villagers lived together in harmony. They celebrated each other's lives and loves, and mourned their deaths together. The simplicity and hardship associated with rural life meant that a harmonious life assured their survival.

The Greek protagonists in The *Embroiderer* were from the upper classes, educated and politically aware of events taking place in the Ottoman Empire. The same could not be said for the villagers throughout Anatolia. Life moved at a slower pace and news came via caravan trains that passed through the villages. Very few knew about events taking place in the wider world and the impact they would have on their lives, especially the Great War and its aftermath. As history has shown, time and time again, once political upheavals and wars gather momentum, they are as unstoppable as a river in flood. *The Carpet Weaver of Uşak* is their story.

A Note about Carpet Weaving in Anatolia

Carpet weaving was Turkey's second most important industry after tobacco, until its demise due to the Great War and the Asia Minor conflict, which devastated it on a number of levels.

For centuries, the finest Turkish carpets graced the palaces and grand homes of the wealthy in Europe. Many of these came to be known as Holbein carpets through the paintings of Hans Holbein and other eminent artists. Most were made in and around Uşak and are also known as Uşak carpets. The "bird" and lozenge motifs are typical of Uşak carpets. Persian carpets were not as widely exported until relatively recently.

Since Byzantium times, the Europeans in Constantinople, or Levantines, as they are more commonly known, benefitted from "capitulations" and paid little tax. It was through these commercial interests that carpet weaving prospered. Constantinople and Smyrna became the export and warehousing centres, but it was the area around Uşak that made the carpets. The hand-loom weavers in the carpet factories were mostly Greek and Armenian women. During the Great War, the Armenian women were the first to leave, followed by the Greeks in the summer of 1922. The majority of Turkish weavers worked from home, practising the traditional skills and knowledge inherited from their ancestors who migrated to Anatolia from Asia

The industry never recovered its prominent status and was not helped by further advances in modern carpet weaving technology, shifting trade policies, and the changing role of women in Turkish society. In the last few decades, concerted government efforts have been made to help re-establish the carpet industry, in particular, high end, quality carpets.

Acknowledgments

I am grateful to a number of people for their help and kindness on this journey.

My thanks to Deanna Wedow, for sharing her great-grandfather's story. Deanna's family come from Asia Minor, and it was she who gave me the inspiration for the Fountain of the Sun and Moon in my novel. Her great-grandfather, Yianni Helios, was from the village of Meli (*Honey* in Greek) in the province of Izmir. Meli no longer exists under that name, and today is a ghost town, reminiscent of many of the old Greek villages throughout Turkey. All that remains are the broken down walls and the fountain that once stood in the centre of the vil-

lage. This fountain is known as the Fountain of Heliou, denoting that it was built as a gift by Yianni Helios, owner of a local coffee shop, who dedicated it to the community. The philanthropic act of dedicating something for the good of the community in one's name was a common practice for wealthy people throughout the entire Ottoman Empire. Such a pious act guaranteed they would be remembered in a prayer. Yianni's fountain shows that this was not just a Muslim tradition, but one acted on by all religions. Deanna's daughter is named Melina, in honour of the village.

I am greatly indebted to Sebnem E. Sanders who has been a mentor to me on all things Turkish. Through our shared interest on Turkey, its history and culture, especially the Asia Minor conflict, we have developed a deep friendship that has provided us with many pleasurable hours of discussion. It was Sebnem who pointed out the difference between city and village names and the manner in which people are addressed, all of which has added authenticity to the novel. All this would have been familiar to the Greeks of Anatolia.

Special thanks to my Greek agent, Evangelia Avloniti of Ersilia Literary Agency, and Eleni Kekropoulou and her staff at Oceanos-Enalios publications, for believing in me.

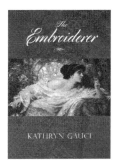

ALSO BY THE AUTHOR

The Embroiderer

1822: During one of the bloodiest massacres of The Greek War of Independence, a child is born to a woman of legendary beauty in the Byzantine monastery of Nea Moni on the Greek island of Chios. The subsequent decades of bitter struggle between Greeks and Turks simmer to a head when the Greek army invades Turkey in 1919. During this time, Dimitra Lamartine arrives in Smyrna and gains fame and fortune as an embroiderer to the elite of Ottoman society. However it is her grand-daughter Sophia, who takes the business to great heights only to see their world come crashing down with the outbreak of The Balkan Wars, 1912-13. In 1922, Sophia begins a new life in Athens but the memory of a dire prophecy once told to her grandmother about a girl with flaming red hair begins to haunt her with devastating consequences.

1972: Eleni Stephenson is called to the bedside of her dying aunt in Athens. In a story that rips her world apart, Eleni discovers the chilling truth behind her family's dark past plunging her into the shadowy world of political intrigue, secret societies and espionage where families and friends are torn apart and where a belief in superstition simmers just below the surface.

Set against the mosques and minarets of Asia Minor and the ruins of ancient Athens, *The Embroiderer* is a gripping saga of love and loss, hope and despair, and of the extraordinary courage of women in the face of adversity.

The Embroiderer is also available in Greek.

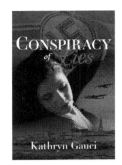

Conspiracy of Lies

A powerful account of one woman's struggle to balance her duty to her country and a love she knows will ultimately end in tragedy.

1940. With the Germans about to enter Paris, Claire Bouchard flees France for England. Two years later she is recruited by the Special Operations Executive and sent back into occupied France to work alongside the Resistance. Working undercover as a teacher in Brittany, Claire accidentally befriends the wife of the German Commandant of Rennes and the blossoming friendship is about to become a dangerous mission.

Knowing that thousands of lives depended on her actions, Claire begins a double life as a Gestapo Commandant's mistress in order to retrieve vital information for the Allied Invasion of France, but ghosts from her past make the deception more painful than she could have imagined.

Part historical, part romance and part thriller, *Conspiracy of Lies* takes us on a journey through occupied France, from the picturesque villages of rural Brittany to the glittering dinner parties of the Nazi Elite, in a story of courage, heartbreak and secrecy.

Seraphina's Song

"If I knew then, dear reader, what I know now, I should have turned on my heels and left. But no, instead, I stood there transfixed on the beautiful image of Seraphina. In that moment my fate was sealed."

Dionysos Mavroulis is a man without a future; a man who embraces destiny and risks everything for love.

A refugee from Asia Minor, he escapes Smyrna in 1922 disguised as an old woman. Alienated and plagued by feelings of remorse, he spirals into poverty and seeks solace in the hashish dens around Piraeus.

Hitting rock bottom, he meets Aleko, an accomplished bouzouki player. Recognising in the impoverished refugee a rare musical talent, Aleko offers to teach him the bouzouki.

Dionysos' hope for a better life is further fuelled when he meets Seraphina — the singer with the voice of a nightingale — at Papazoglou's Taverna. From the moment he lays eyes on her, his fate is sealed.

Set in Piraeus, Greece during the 1920's and 30's, *Seraphina's Song* is a haunting and compelling story of hope and despair, and of a love stronger than death.

AUTHOR BIOGRAPHY

Kathryn Gauci was born in Leicestershire, England, and studied textile design at Loughborough College of Art and Design, and carpet design and technology at Kidderminster College of Art and Design. After graduating, Kathryn spent a year in Vienna, Austria before moving to Greece where she worked as a carpet designer in Athens for six years. There followed another brief period in New Zealand before eventually settling in Melbourne, Australia.

Before turning to writing full-time, Kathryn ran her own textile design studio in Melbourne for over fifteen years, work which she enjoyed tremendously as it allowed her the luxury of travelling worldwide, often taking her off the beaten track and exploring other cultures. *The Embroiderer* is her first novel; a culmination of those wonderful years of design and travel, and especially of those glorious years in her youth living and working in Greece.

Website: www.kathryngauci.com